FORWARD
IN
FAITH

HOW TO PLAN & PREPARE FOR SUCCESSFUL PASTORAL TRANSITION

DR. JASON M. MOSELEY

Published by So It Is Written, LLC
Detroit, MI
SoItIsWritten.net

Forward in Faith: How to Plan & Prepare for Successful Pastoral Transition
Copyright © 2024 by Dr. Jason M. Moseley

Edited by: So It Is Written – www.SoItIsWritten.net

Formatting: Ya Ya Ya Creative – YaYaYaCreative@gmail.com

ISBN: 979-8-9912588-2-1

LCCN: 2024919873

PRINTED AND BOUND IN THE UNITED STATES OF AMERICA

DEDICATION

To my wife, Dr. Anita: Honey, we have been doing life together for a long time, and we have made it every step of the way. You, ma'am, are God's grace in human form. I love you with all of who I am and everything that I have!

To my children, Jeremiah, Caleb and Bella: Mom and I have only wanted to show you that, no matter what, you are able to finish strong. I can only ask God to ensure that you have received the lesson and will do what is necessary for your own lives. Thank you for sharing your dad.

I also want to dedicate this work in memory of my beloved mother who has transitioned from this life to glory eternal, Ms. Clarice L. Johnson. Mommy, you were supposed to be my editor when all of this was over, but God had other plans. Thank you for always being a phone call away and lovingly sharing with me as best you could. I love you from the top of my heart and I pray that I continue to make you proud.

FOREWORD

O ften in Olympic track and field competitions, there is an event known as the relay race. This event features a team of athletes running predetermined distances where runners in the same lane are strategically positioned to navigate the team to victory by passing a baton to the next runner. In order to continue the race at the optimum level, it requires skill, grace and execution on the part of the current runner to transfer the baton to the next runner smoothly and efficiently. The precision of the handoff is critical to the victory, no matter how well the runners run. The goal is a smooth transition without interruption

There is no *success* without *succession*. The reality remains that we all live in the shadow of replacement. However, our institutions, especially the church, are in danger of hanging in the balance without the intentionality of smooth leadership transition. We must revolutionize our thinking toward long-term viability and impact. An ethos of wanting to "see beyond me" must be established so that faith communities cease to exist in the vacuum of personality alone.

In this exciting work, Dr. Jason M. Moseley underscores the mandate of succession to more faith forward by offering a critical template for its necessity and planning. Dr. Moseley reminds us to prepare to perpetuate growth in perpetuity by being prescriptive and intentional. The bricks with which we build today must become the foundations for growth and advancement tomorrow. Let this book provoke your "big picture" thinking as we imagine the future of the church. Share this treatise on pastoral succession as a template for smooth transition. Allow Dr. Moseley's assessment to help guide the facilitation of processes as the Holy Spirit continues to choose and anoint leadership.

Move faith forward!

Bishop Edgar L. Vann, II
Second Ebenezer Church
Detroit, Michigan

ACKNOWLEDGMENTS

*"Without God, I would be nothing. Without God,
I would fail. Without God, my life would be drifting,
like a ship without a sail."*

*Thank you, Lord, for being my strength, shield and comforter.
Thank you for teaching me how to run my own race.*

*I am thankful for the encouragement of so many
who have shared with me in different capacities.
I don't take it for granted.*

TABLE OF CONTENTS

Introduction

Seasons of pastoral transition bring with it the full accompaniment of hurt, pain, remorse, joy, and sometimes division within the church. Healing and wholeness, especially in the Black church, is often an afterthought.

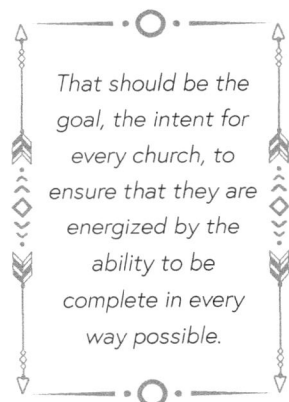

That should be the goal, the intent for every church, to ensure that they are energized by the ability to be complete in every way possible.

Healing and wholeness are words that are not well received in the Black church when associated with interchurch conflict, hurt and pain. Although the Black church associates these words with spiritual health, they have little meaning when trouble arises in the church. However, healing and wholeness are essential to sustainability and vitality in all congregations. That should be the goal, the intent for every church, to ensure that they are energized by the ability to be complete in every way possible. No conflict should be able to take over what God is doing in His church. The structure ought to be of such that the church, more specifically the Black church, moves according to Galatians 6:1 where it says, *"If anyone is overtaken in a fault, you who are spiritual should restore in a spirit of meekness."*

Conversations are necessary. Motives must be pure. Intentions must be sincere. Hearts must be poised toward solidarity, unity and restoration. If the church doesn't stand as a viable example of coming together, and not allowing offenses to drive a wedge within the ranks, is there really hope for the world? If the church doesn't stand true, if it doesn't provide a way of escape from the mundane, futile, trivial and silly arguments that we sometimes find ourselves in, what can be assumed as to how the world will handle what's going on?

The church is still the sample of the example that the Lord restores, heals, reconciles and brings together those things and those people who are able to work together, to be effective, and to provide meaningful ministry to the totality of men, women, boys and girls. It is through pastoral transition that we receive the continuance of order, the continuance of faith, the continuance of pouring, receiving what was on the way to what's next.

In these pages, we will go on a journey. We will see a snapshot of what has been. We will discuss what is presently being experienced, and the favorable future we all can look forward to in faith as we follow a God-given model of transition. In this model, the church at-large will be healthy, formidable, powerful and pertinent to serve this present age in excellence, which is our calling to fulfill in Jesus Christ to the glory of God by the power and fruitful assistance of the Holy Spirit.

HEALTHY EXITS

saiah 49:15 says, "*Can a woman forget her baby who nurses at her breast? Can she withhold compassion from the child she has borne? Even if mothers were to forget, I could never forget you! Look, I have inscribed your name on my palms; your walls are constantly before me.*"[1] Psalm 27:10 says, "*Even if my father and mother abandoned me, the Lord would take me in.*" Psalm 9:10-11 says, "*Your loyal followers trust in you, for you, Lord, do not abandon those who seek your help.*"

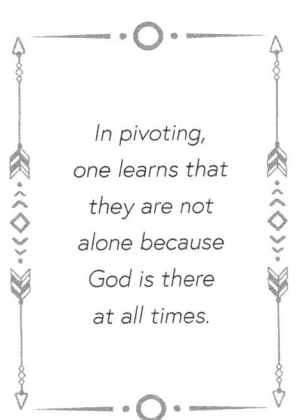

In pivoting, one learns that they are not alone because God is there at all times.

The prophet Isaiah and the psalmist both speak to the issue of abandonment. Both writers express the importance of the fact that God is present and near, no matter who leaves us. Through these writers, we see comfort and consolation during a time of loneliness and abandonment—

---

[1] Isaiah 49:15-16, NASB. Unless otherwise indicated, all biblical references in this document are taken from the New American Standard version of the Bible, NASB.

whether it be by a mother or father, extended family member, society or even the church.

Abandonment means to be deserted, neglected or stranded, either for a long period of time or permanently. It is necessary to understand the words of the prophet Isaiah and David to ensure one does not succumb to the feeling of abandonment. Through it, however, one should learn how to pivot in spite of it. In pivoting, one learns that they are not alone because God is there at all times. He helps us navigate our emotions during our time of abandonment. He reminds us and reassures us of His presence. His presence is protection. His presence is peace in the midst of pain and peril. It is when we find this peace that we are able to function properly. Without faltering, we are able to accomplish the things that have been set before us—whether it's in the four walls of a church building or in the marketplace.

This is the launching pad for me as a man and a leader. My goal is to assist those who have and continue to feel abandoned. In order for them to move past where they are, they have to forgive where they have been, who they have been, how they have been, and what direction they were going. Throughout my life, I understood and yet understand the importance of being delivered from the trauma-infused focus of abandonment. I learned to cultivate a sense of forward thinking that leads to forward progression in both my mind and actions. As a result, I now focus on the strengths I received through my weakness of abandonment. I do not allow the past to interrupt the favorable future. I decided to channel my emotions in a different fashion.

This synergy is the basis for how my personal life intersects with that of the ministry God allows me to lead in Detroit. Both have pasts that haunt the present, or at least try to. However, this is not the end-all and be-all for either of us. It was Bishop T. D. Jakes who said, "If you do not make peace with your past, you cannot stand effective in your present or future." There must be a reckoning with what one has lost. So, there is a later victory with you and I being able to use what we have been given. The synergy allows my ministry and personal context to collide, illuminating the distinct, similar characteristics that each has with one another.

For the last few years, there has been a church served through the pastorate called Faith Church. To say that it is a tremendous blessing to serve is an understatement. The ability to move and interact with the congregation, and the community in which the church is located, is a delicate blessing and honor. There has been ministry exhibited that has groomed and taught people to grow beyond where they are, to learn to appreciate and honor leadership again, while also serving God with a spirit of excellence and living their lives filled with faith in every area possible.

It is my firm belief that if the people of God are led by example, and they are ushered into a new leadership style while still honoring what has been, it will cultivate a sense of wholeness and success for what is to come for the ministry. This applies not just to the brick-and-mortar building, but the individuals that frequent the building. The ability to forgive what has been, cultivate what is, and build on the foundation that is present is the plan and course of

People are people. God is God. Life should be handled accordingly based on that fact.

action. If there is no teaching that will assist in this effort, things will remain the same and this local church may never experience all that God has for us.

When I think of Faith Church, I believe that the church should be a well-oiled machine, ready to serve this present age, which is our calling to fulfill. It does not mean it does not come without issues, or problems. It does mean that the control is not in the problem, but the solutions that will come from the righteous God and the hearts and minds of people who are whole and secure. The church that deals with the effects of emotional disturbance and feelings of abandonment can draw from areas that help deliver and set them free. The church should be able to stand on and glean from biblical and theological foundations for growth and maturity in areas of emotional stability and the mindset to move on. Faith Church, as a whole, believes in restoration, reconciliation, and healing, and a pursuit of all three with persistency, consistency, and reverence for who God is, while recognizing the weakness or ills of people. This is significant because it keeps everything in perspective. People are people. God is God. Life should be handled accordingly based on that fact.

Ministerially, I work in a context that, as a whole, feels as if they have been abandoned by the previous administration and leadership of the church which no longer serves the church presently. However, long before the official leaving, some parishioners felt as though they had clocked out already. He wasn't preaching like normal. It didn't seem as though he was giving it his best, especially if the congregation wasn't what he desired it to be. To sum it all up, there were some things that transpired in the church on the administration's way out because the church was in such bad shape that they weren't able to adequately respond in the affirmative to what was desired, due to declining membership. As a result, the people *were* hurt, and if truth be told, they are *still* hurt.

In this instance, we see an administration who has already left the building. However, to add insult to injury, they take the church and devise a plan to make them pay for something that was legitimately out of their control. So many emotions and thought processes derived from such an ordeal. So, you have a church that desires to grow from where they are and to rise out of the ashes to be all God has called them to be. The church is also in a financial bind because of misplaced priorities. Now, there is a devilish plan in the works on top of all of the other things the church is fiscally responsible for. To top it off, the church has to recruit a new pastor and church leader in the midst of all that's going on.

Unfortunately, this has been the experience for many churches in North America. Ideally, there must be a succession plan in place, which ensures smooth transition and succession from one administration to the next. Even with existing problems, there should be a way to navigate those problems so that the people and the leadership are able to adequately assess where they are and follow the proposed plan to get where they need to be. In my context, and so many others, there is a need for restorative practices

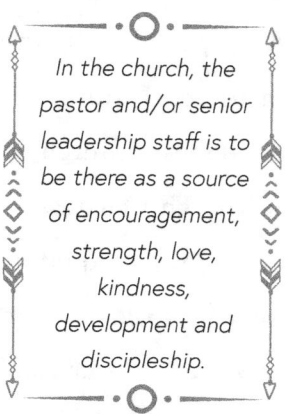

In the church, the pastor and/or senior leadership staff is to be there as a source of encouragement, strength, love, kindness, development and discipleship.

that help the people of the church move forward without holding a grudge or allowing emotions to get the best of them. As a result, they learn how to forgive as Christ has forgiven us. Built to foster hope, faith and forward progression, the church needs to find a way to do the same for herself.

No one likes to feel abandoned. No one likes to feel like they are left to fend for themselves. In the church, the pastor and/or senior leadership staff is to be there as a source of encouragement, strength, love, kindness, development and discipleship. No doubt when it seems as if that is not there, it brings pain and anguish to the hearts of those who trusted and relied on that pastor and/or leadership. There is no church or entity that is able to move beyond where they are if they cannot adequately process the feelings and emotions of what was. As a result, the people suffer. The community in which the church resides suffers. The next generation suffers because there is no reconciliation nor an adaptation to a better structure, loving leadership, and the tools needed to heal and be successful in the next stage of ministry.

Reflecting on my childhood experiences, I can acquiesce with the notion of feeling abandoned. No doubt, I love my mother. I believe she loved me, as well. However, I also believe, like most, that love should translate with more than just words. Love is best shown through consistent action. Growing up, it seemed as if she chose other things over her children. It was almost like she did not know how to adequately care for us. However, I also believe that experiencing this was what I needed to make sure I did some things a certain way to not fall into the same trap in other relationships. In addition to that, the feelings that I experienced became the catalyst to a better relationship with my mom. It was an ordeal that challenged my way of thinking and, ultimately, my actions. What I expect from someone else is what I need to give, whether they change or not. That's what it means to be whole, mature and growing in every area.

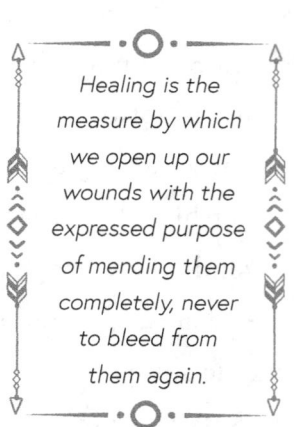

Healing is the measure by which we open up our wounds with the expressed purpose of mending them completely, never to bleed from them again.

The congregants as a whole may not desire a better relationship with the previous administration. However, going through such an ordeal teaches them what to do and what not to do when it comes to the present pastor or the next. This affects the present leadership of the church, as well as the future. Not allowing what has been to be the driving force is critical. However, understanding that living from a whole place puts them in a place of peace and longevity for proper fruit to flow from this ministry. It's time for the culture to change. It's time to allow the new culture to be effective in moving the church forward, to become more understanding, focused, progressive, powerful, properly influential, and settled.

From both my personal and spiritual contexts, we see that healing needs to take place. Healing is the measure by which we open up our wounds with the expressed purpose of mending them completely, never to bleed from them again. It is my plan to reach out to those in my context to see what they need to ensure that healing takes place. What are some areas that need healing? When did you know that those areas of your life were affected? How do you view the church based on what has transpired? What are you willing to do to experience total healing and restoration? These are just a few of the questions I will ask to compile a step-by-step guide or manual to complete healing and wholeness in the church after experiencing transition in leadership.

It has been said that, "A true leader does not create separation; a true leader will bring people together." I will add to that and say that a true leader who sees dissension and discord will avail themselves to a proper protocol and establish a standard to abide by that will influence their congregants and the church at-large to transition well, with purpose, on purpose, for a successful process. My goal is to create a process by which the church and present leadership can move forward in a healthy, maintained and fruitful way.

This content is not just for the present leadership, but for those to come. The church itself is a viable institution that will go through many transitions for as long as it exists. There should be a viable, documented solution in place that will serve as a model that the church is able to build upon as time progresses.

OBEDIENCE IN TRANSITION

Biblical Foundations

The biblical foundation validating the issues this project deals with is Joshua 1:1-18. Joshua's historical and literary contexts will be discussed as a framework for the exegetical analysis. These contextual analyses will investigate Joshua's authorship, date, purpose, and composition. A verse-by-verse analysis section comprising grammatical and syntactical details will follow.

Additionally, the book of Joshua has a few major themes, as noted by most scholars. Instead of devoting a special section to those themes, I will focus on the themes found in my selected pericope. Finally, I will conclude my research with a summary section and leadership principles that preview how the biblical pericope converges with my final project.

Contextual Analysis[2]

Joshua is the sixth book of the Bible and is placed at a critical juncture in the biblical story. It is seen as a canonical

---

[2] Details on context can be found in the introduction section of most commentaries.

bridge. On the one hand, Joshua closes the book on the story of Israel's origins. Israel's story begins in Genesis 12, when the Lord directs Abram to leave his kindred and his family and "go to the land I will show you." The rest of Genesis is propelled by this promise of a land and a place to live with God. When the Lord comes to Moses in Exodus 3, one of the first things God says to him is that He has heard the cry of His people, and He has come down, and now He is ready to bring His people into the land that He promised to their ancestors. Therefore, the book of Joshua completes this story by relating how Israel indeed came into the land and took possession of it. That is exemplified by a summary toward the end of the book. Joshua 21:43 reads, *"Thus the LORD gave to Israel all the land that he swore to their ancestors that he would give them; and having taken possession of it, they settled there."*[3]

Joshua, however, also opens the book with the story of Israel's life in the land. It establishes some of the main trajectories, motifs and themes that will configure that story from its beginning in Joshua to its end in Israel's expulsion from the land. Joshua 23:15 says, *"It shall come about that just as all the good words which the LORD your God spoke to you have come upon you, so the LORD will bring upon you all the threats, until He has destroyed you from off this good land which the LORD your God has given you."* Joshua,

---

[3] Richard S. Hess, "Joshua: An Introduction and Commentary," vol. 6, *Tyndale Old Testament Commentaries* (Downers Grove, IL: InterVarsity Press, 1996), 21.

therefore, looks ahead to the ending of this story, which leaves Israel outside of the land once again. Again, it is represented by a short statement from 2 Kings 24:20: *"Indeed Jerusalem and Judah so angered the Lord that he expelled them from his presence."*

The name of the book (Joshua) and the main character's name is a valid and appropriate name for the content and the impulse of the story itself. *Yehoshua* in Hebrew means "Yahweh saves" or even something like "Yahweh brings victory." Yahweh does indeed bring victory to Israel in this book. In so doing, establishes Israel in a place where it can now enjoy the life which God has promised and intends for His people.[4]

Division prevails amid experts on the authorship of Joshua. The Talmud credits Joshua for writing most of the book, with Eleazar, the son of Aaron, recording Joshua's death.[5] Some Jewish medieval expositors also posit Joshua as the author while ascribing a later hand to 15:14-19 and 19:37.[6] Based on the expression "until this day" (Joshua 4:9; 5:9; 7:26), other Jewish medieval scholars believed Samuel to have written Joshua.[7]

---

[4]   Hess, "Joshua: An Introduction and Commentary," 21.

[5]   Marten H. Woudstra, "The Book of Joshua," *The New International Commentary on the Old Testament* (Grand Rapids, MI: Wm E. Eerdmans Publishing Co., 1981), 5.

[6]   Woudstra, "The Book of Joshua," 5.

[7]   Woudstra, "The Book of Joshua," 5. Additionally, almost all scholars mention the conventional inspiration behind writing the book—As the events in Joshua unfold, doubtless, the main message to the readers is that the conquest is a gift from God.

The primary purpose of Joshua is to outline Israel's conquest, distribution and settlement of the promised land. In Genesis 15, God promised to give His people a land. With the death of Moses, and Joshua inaugurated as Israel's new leader, the time arrived. Significant theological overtones emerge from the background as Israel's "prophetical" history unfolds: 1) God has not reneged on his covenant; 2) The conquest is undoubtedly a gift from God.

Exegesis

Joshua 1:1 says, *Now it came about after the death of Moses the servant of the LORD, that the LORD spoke to Joshua the son of Nun, Moses' servant, saying.*

The book of Joshua commences as a continuation of previous events. The literal translation of the beginning of the verse would read, "And it happened, after the death of Moses the servant of the Lord, the Lord said to Joshua..."[8] The notion of continuation is continued by recounting Moses' death in Deuteronomy 34 1-8. Moses had led Israel for forty years. He was a towering figure in the life of Israel, (See Deuteronomy 34: 10-12) and doubtlessly, his death could have crippled Israel's hopes of receiving their

---

[8] David M. Howard, Jr. "Joshua," vol. 5. *The New American Commentary* (Nashville, TN: Broadman & Holman Publishers, 1998).

promise. Yet, God proves that his promise is not nullified; Israel will possess the land with Joshua at the helm.[9]

As Joshua is commissioned to lead Israel, it is no incident that he is portrayed as a worthy successor of Moses. The author makes this abundantly clear with the phrase "Joshua the son of Nun, Moses' servant." Earlier biblical references such as Numbers 27:15-23 and Deuteronomy 3:21 -22; 31:1-8 evinces Joshua prophetically as Moses' successor. Exodus 24:13; 33:11 and Numbers 11:28 parallel Moses' and Joshua's relationship to God and Moses' relationship.[10] While Joshua receives the high commission as Moses' successor, for most of the book, he will carry the title "Moses' Servant," indicating that such a noble title comes with unwavering faithfulness tc Yahweh,[11] which Joshua must ultimately demonstrate.

Additionally, the variation of the Hebrew words *mĕšārēt* and *'ebed* differentiates the relationship between Moses to the Lord and Joshua to Moses.[12] Nevertheless, it is a misnomer to speak of Moses' and Joshua's relationship in terms of superiority and subordination, as it is the tradition of some scholars. At this point in the life of Israel, Moses' quality of leadership stands as unrivaled due solely to the

---

[9] It is important to note that Moses' death is reminiscent of his disobedience.

[10] Hess, "Joshua: An Introduction and Commentary," 73.

[11] Hess, "Joshua: An Introduction and Commentary," 56.

[12] Hess, "Joshua: An Introduction and Commentary," 74.

uniqueness of his God-commissioned assignment and due to his physical, ethical or spiritual advancement.

Joshua 1:2-5 says,

Moses My servant is dead; now therefore arise, cross this Jordan, you and all this people, to the land which I am giving to them, to the sons of Israel. "Every place on which the sole of your foot treads, I have given it to you, just as I spoke to Moses. "From the wilderness and this Lebanon, even as far as the great river, the river Euphrates, all the land of the Hittites, and as far as the Great Sea toward the setting of the sun will be your territory. "No man will be able to stand before you all the days of your life. Just as I have been with Moses, I will be with you; I will not fail you or forsake you.

These verses establish a significant synopsis of the book of Joshua. Verse two details the crossing of the Jordan. Verse three previews the conquest of 5:13-12:24. Verse four overviews the distribution of the land found in 13:1-22:34. The concept, "...all the days of Joshua's life" in verse five is expanded during the end of Joshua's life in the book's last two chapters.

Verse two opens with God specifically referring to Moses as His servant, a repeated notion from verse one. Various interpretations have been developed from such repetitions. David Howard sees the repetition as assuring the readers that God was undoubtedly committed to fulling His promises.[13] According to Woudstra, the repetition establishes the occasion for God's command to cross the Jordan into Canaan.[14] Bratcher and Newman highlight that the repeated notion solidifies Moses as God's servant.[15] These slight angles convey the polyvalent nature of such a phrase against the differencing of meaning.

Subsequently, there is a command to cross the Jordan. Joshua, Israel and all those familiar with the geography knew the degree of difficulty of the command.[16] Woudstra describes the geographical condition as such:

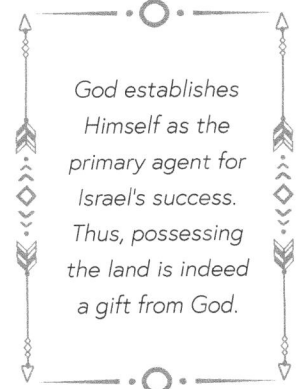

God establishes Himself as the primary agent for Israel's success. Thus, possessing the land is indeed a gift from God.

"The river Jordan had a separating rather than a connecting function, running through a deep gorge which may be called the earth's deepest valley. The Jordan flows into the Dead Sea, which lies 1286 feet below sea level. The river runs through a wider trough called the Ghor, within which is a narrower depression of one hundred feet or more in depth, forming the actual

[13] Howard, "Joshua," vol. 5, 75.

[14] Woudstra, *The Book of Joshua*, 58.

[15] Robert G. Bratcher and Barclay Moon Newman. *A Translator's Handbook on the Book of Joshua*, UBS Handbook Series (London, UK; New York, NY: United Bible Societies, 1983).

[16] Woudstra, *The Book of Joshua*, 57.

river bottom. In addition to these forbidding features the absolute level of the river valley is greatly enhanced by the mountains on both sides. The slopes are generally steep and sudden, sometimes forming huge precipices. Also note 3:15, which points to the river's swollen condition at the time of the crossing. Thus, the miracle of the Lord's giving of the land is anticipated effectively by the writer's recalling of the Lord's command."[17]

Moses' death is repeated to reinforce a changing of the guard from Moses' to Joshua's leadership. Israel will not possess the land due to them merely engineering a triumphant military strategy. God establishes Himself as the primary agent for Israel's success. Thus, possessing the land is indeed a gift from God. The gift motif is supported in verses 2 and 3 with two forms of the verb "give." In verse 2, "give" is expressed as an "already-not yet" occurrence; verse 3 implies a completed action. As a result, the gift motif reveals a two-fold aspect to Israel taking the land—God gives and instructs—Israel must act upon God's instructions.

Thus, inheriting God's promise is contingent on all of Israel acting according to His instructions. Such is evinced by the plural "you" and "your" in verse 3 where God shifted from speaking to Joshua exclusively to including all of

---

[17] Woudstra, *The Book of Joshua*, 57.

Israel. Bratcher & Newman note that the inclusive stroke provided by the phrase "you and all this people (v.2)" may function counterproductively by implying that Joshua and Israel are separate subjects of the inherited promise.[18]

In verse four, the author advances to sketch the boundaries of Israel's conquest in broad strokes. These general descriptions cover territories in all four directions—north, south, east, and west. First mentioned are the southern and northern boundaries—the wilderness in the south and the Lebanon in the north. The wilderness is a general term that likely refers in the Old Testament to all barren areas,[19] or more precisely, the cultivated land of Palestine to the south and east.[20] The Lebanon is more or less present-day Lebanon. The phrasing "this Lebanon" may accentuate the not visible aspect of the land in relation to where the Israelites were located.[21] Following the north and south boundaries are the east and west. The Euphrates River precisely constitutes the northeastern border; however, in biblical geography, it is synonymous with the eastern border.[22] The Great Sea of the West represents the Mediterranean Sea.[23]

---

[18] Bratcher and Barclay Moon Newman. *A Translator's Handbook on the Book of Joshua*, 12.

[19] Howard, "Joshua," vol. 5, 81.

[20] Woudstra, *The Book of Joshua*, 58.

[21] Howard, "Joshua," vol. 5, 81.

[22] Ibid.

[23] Woudstra, *The Book of Joshua*, 59.

Verse five is the spiritual zenith of the first portion of God's commission to Joshua. It is a warming assurance to Joshua that his and the Israelite's efforts will not be in vain, and that God would be present through the entire ordeal. The ethos of the promise is realized by assuring Joshua the same way he assured Moses (cf. Dt 7:24). God's promise initiates the answer to whether Joshua's leadership would square up with Moses' leadership resume.[24] Moreover, the words, "I will be with you" are meaningfully reminiscent of God's name and was inextricably integrated with the idea of his keeping covenant with his people.[25]

Joshua 1:6-9 says,

Be strong and courageous, for you shall give this people possession of the land which I swore to their fathers to give them. "Only be strong and very courageous; be careful to do according to all the law which Moses My servant commanded you; do not turn from it to the right or to the left, so that you may have success wherever you go. "This book of the law shall not depart from your mouth, but you shall meditate on it day and night, so that you may be careful to do according to all that is written in it; for then you will make your way prosperous, and then you will have success. "Have I not commanded you? Be strong and courageous! Do not tremble or be dismayed, for the LORD your God is with you wherever you go.

---

[24] Howard, "Joshua," vol. 5, 82.

[25] Ibid.

Verse six shifts from the promises of the first half of the address to the premises that Joshua must adhere.[26] Since God has promised His presence to Joshua (v.5), Joshua is expected to "be strong and courageous." These two ideas are closely related in meaning and ultimately mean that Joshua is to be resilient as he faces challenges of his assignment.[27] The contents of God's charge are not new to Joshua. Moses had previously given Joshua a similar charge in Deuteronomy 1:38; 3:28. The phrase also appears in 1 Chronicles 28:20, where David charges Solomon with building the temple. Once again, the phrase appears in Joshua 10:25, where Joshua encourages Israel to fight against their foe, which is similar to Hezekiah's usage of the phrase as he prepared the people to stand against the Assyrians (2 Chronicles 32:7). These references demonstrate that the phrase can be used in various ways, but it is always connected with God's presence and Him as a pillar.[28]

The repeated command in verse 7 to be "strong and courageous" is directed to Joshua regarding keeping the law. Joshua is to act strictly according to the entire law of Moses. Interestingly, at this point, God is not giving Joshua instructions on military strategy, which accentuates the relationship between spiritual obedience and Joshua's

---

[26] Hess, "Joshua: An Introduction and Commentary," 78.

[27] Howard, "Joshua," vol. 5, 84.

[28] Hess, "Joshua: An Introduction and Commentary," 78.

success.[29] Moreover, Israel needed Joshua to be resolute because their success depended on it. Howard observed: "The need for Joshua to be strong and resolute was acute because he was the instrument for the people to inherit the land. The Hebrew grammatical construction here highlights Joshua himself: if he, of all people, was weak and irresolute, then the cause was in deep trouble."[30]

God advances to establish the method for keeping the law in verse 8. Joshua was to meditate upon the law, day and night. Such meditational practice is different from the Eastern mystic religious idea of meditation. The Old Testament idea of meditation involves: 1) gazing upon God Himself (cf. Psalm 63:6); His works (Psalm 77:12), or His law (Joshua 1:8; Psalm 1:2); and 2) an activity done aloud, such as reciting the law.

The author closes the first section with another exhortation to "be strong and courageous." Once more, this is more than meaningless repetition. God assures Joshua of His presence and participation with each reiteration as Joshua leads Israel into the promised land.

Joshua 1:10-11 says,

Then Joshua commanded the officers of the people, saying,
"Pass through the midst of the camp and command the people,

---

[29] Howard, "Joshua," vol. 5, 85.

[30] Ibid.

saying, 'Prepare provisions for yourselves, for within three days
you are to cross this Jordan, to go in to possess the land which
the LORD your God is giving you, to possess it.

At this point, the tone of the passage shifts from God
speaking with Joshua to Joshua speaking with the people.
Here Joshua assumes the leadership role assigned to him.
Joshua's first order is for the officers to pass through the
midst of the camp and command the people to prepare
provisions.[31] The verbal phrase "go through" is identical to
the verb used in verse two. As a verb of action, it establishes
the critical activity in the opening chapters.[32] The text does
not give specifics about the provisions. Gathering provisions
likely entails getting food since the manna had already ceased
to fall.[33] Nevertheless, martial specifics are not of concern at
this point. The main point is that Israel is on the brink of
initiating taking the land (cf. Deuteronomy 3:18; 4:5, 14).

The word "provision" or "supplies" appears in Genesis
42:25 and 45:21 as Joseph provides his brothers with
provisions for their return to Canaan.[34] Furthermore, the
lack of preparing provisions is pictured during the exodus

---

[31] For discussion on the identity of the officers, see Ex 5:6-19; Num 11:16; Dt 1:15, 20:5-9, 29:10, 31:28; Jos 8:33, 23:2, 24:1.

[32] The offices of the people could be the foremen used by Pharoah for extra work (Ex 5:6-19). They are also found in Numbers 11:16 for which they are included in the seventy elders chosen by Moses. Furthermore, they show up in Deuteronomy 1:15 as Israel Judges.

[33] Woudstra, *The Book of Joshua*, 64.

[34] Hess, "Joshua: An Introduction and Commentary," 83.

where the Israelites took dough with yeast, resulting in baking unleavened bread.[35] Moreover, the exodus and the conquest are brought together by the word "provision" while also showing distinctions.

The first crossing was done with haste, while the Jordan crossing was done with sufficient preparation.[36] Moreover, the Jordan crossing conveys a ceremonial act of worship. It takes on a ritual aroma evinced by such repetition of "cross the Jordan ... the land I/the Lord your God am/is giving to them/you," while the exodus event portrays Israel fleeing from their enemy.[37]

Joshua 1:12-15

To the Reubenites and to the Gadites and to the half-tribe of Manasseh, Joshua said, "Remember the word which Moses the servant of the Lord commanded you, saying, "The Lord your God gives you rest and will give you this land.' "Your wives, your little ones, and your cattle shall remain in the land which Moses gave you beyond the Jordan, but you shall cross before your brothers in battle array, all your valiant warriors, and shall help them, until the Lord gives your brothers rest, as He gives you, and they also possess the land which the Lord your God is giving them. Then you shall return to your own land,

---

[35] Ibid.

[36] Ibid.

[37] Ibid.

and possess that which Moses the servant of the Lord gave you
beyond the Jordan toward the sunrise."

Joshua now turns from instructing Israel to speaking to
the Transjordan tribes. Joshua's charge to the tribes is a
fulfillment of an earlier agreement made to Moses. In fact,
verses 13-15 quote Deuteronomy 3:18-20 almost word for
word. Hess underscores the noticeable differences being: 1)
Joshua includes that "God is giving you rest; 2) The
Transjordanian fighters are described as "valiant," while
Deuteronomy describes them as armed for battle; 3)
Deuteronomy recognizes the large number of livestock and
possessions of the people who remained east; and 4) Joshua
includes the phrase, "You are to help your brothers," which
is the driving factor of Joshua's instructions.[38] Nevertheless,
the similarities establish the literary link between the two
and again confirm Joshua's role as Israel's leader.[39]

Joshua's opening line to the Transjordan tribe is prudent
and persuasive. As Joshua speaks to the Transjordan tribes,
he immediately appeals to Moses' commandment to them.
Consequently, the Transjordan tribes are reminded that they
had already received their land authorized by Moses and
made pledges and agreements with Moses.[40] Furthermore,

---

[38] Hess, "Joshua: An Introduction and Commentary," 84.

[39] Ibid.

[40] Ibid, 85.

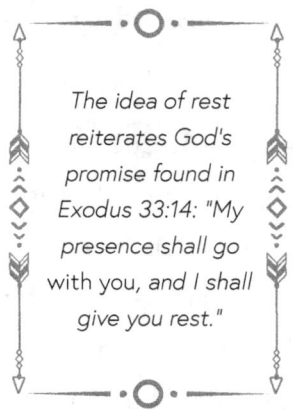

The idea of rest reiterates God's promise found in Exodus 33:14: "My presence shall go with you, and I shall give you rest."

the reiteration of Moses' command and understanding between the Transjordan tribes associates Joshua with Moses, permitting Joshua to speak over them.[41]

Verse 13 gives the first reference to the central theme of "rest" found in the book of Joshua. Mentioned in Numbers 32:20-22 and Deuteronomy 3:18-20, the promise of rest is a gift from God that is inherit to Israel possessing the land.[42] The idea of rest reiterates God's promise found in Exodus 33:14: "My presence shall go *with you,* and I shall give you rest." Hess has noted, "Rest is the goal of the created order in Genesis 1:1-2:3. Israel celebrated it in the Sabbath (Exodus 20:8-11) and associated with the nation's redemption from Egypt."[43]

The language of verse 14 is a cluster of military vocabulary, which up until this point has been deemphasized. Unsure of the exact meaning of the phrase "battle array," the Hebrew word is related to the terms for "five"[44] (hames) and "fifty" (hamissim), and many scholars

---

[41] Besides appealing to the interaction between Moses and the Transjordan tribes, there is no other basis for which Joshua has authority to speak over them.

[42] Howard, "Joshua," vol. 5, 93.

[43] Hess, "Joshua: An Introduction and Commentary," 85.

[44] Howard, "Joshua," vol. 5, 93.

suggest it means something like "ined up in battle array, in groups of fifty...." The term is used synonymously to Exodus 13:18; Judges 7:11; Joshua 4:12; and elsewhere.[45] The phrase "valiant warriors" can also be referred to as "the mighty men of valor." These men were the crème de la crème of the military. They will be pictured in Joshua 8:3 during the ambush of Ai and the battle at Gilgal (Joshua 10:7). Additionally, these men make up the four hundred mighty men of 1 Samuel 22:2 and the six hundred men in 1 Samuel 27:2.

As the section concludes, it is essential to note that the notion of unity is at the center of Joshua's speech to the Transjordan tribes. Verse 15's salient point is that rest may not be enjoyed entirely until the entire nation of Israel achieves it together. The arrangement of the marching formation displays such— "…you shall cross in front of your brothers in battle array."

Joshua 1:16-18 says,

They answered Joshua, saying, "All that you have commanded us we will do, and wherever you send us we will go. "Just as we obeyed Moses in all things, so we will obey you: only may the Lord your God be with you as He was with Moses. "Anyone who rebels against your command and does not obey your words in all that you command him, shall be put

---

[45] Ibid.

to death; only be strong and courageous." Then Joshua the son of Nun sent two men as spies secretly from Shittim, saying, Go, view the land, especially Jericho." So they went and came into the house of a harlot whose name was Rahab, and lodged there.

The final section of chapter one opens with the people responding to Joshua in the affirmative. Precisely who answers Joshua has been discussed among scholars. Hall recognizes that it is the eastern tribes speaking, but holds that the words function representatively.[46] Auld believes verses 16-18 is the response of the local officials, and Howards maintains that both the officials and eastern tribal spokespersons are speaking.[47] Knauf contends that the military leaders or the entire army is speaking.[48] Though it is not wrong to read the response as a representative, the immediate context indicates that it is the voice of the Transjordan tribes representing all others.

Such affirmation from the Transjordan officials would have been warm and encouraging. In that moment, the officers were sure that they would make good on their commitment to Moses—hence the words "all" and "wherever." Furthermore, we have no textual evidence that

---

[46] Trent C. Butler, "Joshua 1–12," edited by Nancy L. deClaissé-Walford, second edition. vol. 7a. *Word Biblical Commentary* (Grand Rapids, MI: Zondervan, 2014), 229.

[47] Butler, "Joshua 1–12," 229.

[48] Ibid.

the officials were insincere. However, Israel's record reflected moments of disobedience. For instance, when Moses brought the laws to the Israelites, they responded, *"All the words which the Lord has spoken we will do!"* (Exodus 24:3, 7). Yet, shortly afterward, Aaron would lead the people in erecting a golden calf (Exodus 32). Such an example, along with a record of complaints and rebellion, may cause suspicion to arise regarding the people's promise.

A contingency appears to follow the warm and confident response of the Transjordan official. The word "only" in verse 17 establishes limits on the complete commitment of the people. Butler renders verse 17b to mean that, for the Transjordan tribe to comply, they must recognize God's presence and Joshua's demonstration of courage. Hess underscores the reversal in verse 17 (i.e., Moses-Joshua-Joshua-Moses); therefore, rejecting it as a limit on their commitment, but rather as confession and prayer that God may be with Joshua as he was with Moses.[49] Similar to Hess, Woudstra reads verse 17 as a blessing to Joshua from the Transjordan officials.

Nevertheless, the word "only," written before an imperfect verb, expresses contrast with what precedes it.[50] Furthermore, when read as a wish, confession, blessing, etc.,

---

[49] Hess, "Joshua: An Introduction and Commentary," 86.

[50] Howard, "Joshua," vol. 5, 95.

the indicative mood of "may" is not taken into account, which confuses the presence of God with Joshua as a wish and not a statement of fact.[51] Therefore, Howard gives the most compelling interpretation, "...Joshua would not be able to rely on the people's obedience—despite their promises! Instead, his success would come from the Lord's presence, not from the people's compliance (or lack of it).[52]

Chapter one concludes with a warning of consequences for those who rebel against Joshua's instructions. With the inclusive "Anyone" at the beginning of verse 18, the author is careful to exclude no one from their responsibility to obey Joshua. Those who act contrary to Joshua's instructions are said to be walking in rebellion. The verb "rebels" occurs only here in Joshua. The phrase, "Anyone who rebels against your command" is found in Scripture only three times, referencing the rebellion of

Since Israel has a proven past of disobeying God during Moses' leadership, it is especially appropriate to give such a warning as Joshua assumes his leadership role.

an earlier generation of Israel. Thus, the current generation likely held Israel's past failures and punishments in their

---

[51] The NIV is an example rendering of v.17b as the people blessing Joshua –"Just as we fully obeyed Moses, so we will obey you. Only may the Lord your God be with you as he was with Moses."

[52] Howard, "Joshua," vol. 5, 95. When deciding between the two dominate ways to interpret v.17b, vocabulary and syntax presents sufficient evidence to read it as a limit placed on Joshua instead of blessing Joshua.

minds while hearing the beginning of verse 18.[53] Since Israel has a proven past of disobeying God during Moses' leadership, it is especially appropriate to give such a warning as Joshua assumes his leadership role. Such sentiment also proves Joshua as Moses' successor since there is a warning against disobeying Joshua as they disobeyed Moses.

Moreover, the author is clear and concise regarding the consequence of disobeying Joshua: "…shall be put to death… ." Here is another motif with past references. As Israel wandered in the wilderness, death was always near whenever they rebelled. Additionally, the consequence of rebellion is so severe that the author frames it in constitutional language. The phrase "shall be put to death" is a legal phrase expressed in various laws sanctioning death.[54] As a reminder to all of God's people that a successful conquest can be realized, the author concludes verse 18a with a fourth and final "only be strong and courageous."[55]

Chapter one begins with the report of the death of Moses, which effectively closes, then, the era of the Pentateuch and tells us that we are in a new time. Although there is continuity, there is now a difference. After the report of the death of Moses, we find four speeches: first, a long speech

---

[53] Israel previous rebellion is mentioned extensively in Deuteronomy 1:26; 9:7,23,24; 31:27.

[54] Hess, "Joshua: An Introduction and Commentary," 86.

[55] Verse 18b is intended to transition the narrative to chapter 2.

from the Lord to Joshua; then a second piece from Joshua to the leaders of Israel; the third speech of Joshua to the tribes of Reuben, Gad and half Manasseh; then a final speech, in which the tribes report to Joshua. Scattered throughout all of these speeches are virtual quotations from Deuteronomy and a reference in the middle of the chapter to "this book of the law," a phrase that is used by Deuteronomy with reference to itself.

Every narrative begins with an exposition that sets up the story and gives us an orientation. By these devices and in this way, the writer of Joshua is starting this story by saying to us, "Remember Deuteronomy and view what takes place as an extension of all that you have read of what Moses has said and what God has communicated to Moses. It is all now going to configure the action that takes place."

The arrangement of God's first speech is interesting in that it gives us a sense of promise and command. God offers Joshua a promise, reminds him of the promise, and then gives him an order. Such a scheme echoes the initial calling of Abraham, but in reverse. When God called Abram in Genesis 12:1–3, God gives, first, a command to Abram to leave his land, his kindred and his home, and to go to the place that God would later show him. Then, God gives him a blessing. Thus, we have the same scheme of command and promise at the beginning of Joshua, but it is now reversed.

God promises now a land to go into, then follows with a command to occupy. Abram left his land in response to a promise and received a blessing. Joshua now enters a land with a promise of blessing and in obedience to a command.

In verses 2-5, God makes several promises. Central of them is the promise of God's presence during the entire conquest. Such promise infuses Joshua's and Israel's courage and provides a sufficient impetus for Israel's obedience to God. Six exhortations follow God's promise to Joshua: Be strong, brave; do not tremble, do not fear, for the Lord your God is with you wherever you go; keep the book of the law in mind; do not lose your way; be very careful.

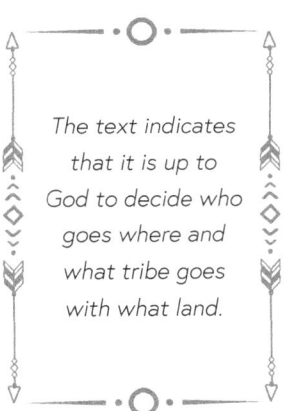

The text indicates that it is up to God to decide who goes where and what tribe goes with what land.

These exhortations direct Joshua toward obedience, courage and resoluteness. Obeying the task ahead requires energy, focus and concentration. In the same way, as He has begun, God ends with a promise of His presence. As the second section of chapter one begins, Joshua gives a brief set of directions to the leaders of Israel, then speaks to the tribes of Reuben, Gad and half Manasseh. He reminds them of an agreement they made with Moses before entering the land. It is recorded in two versions (Numbers 32:1–42; Deuteronomy 3:12–22).

The Transjordan tribes took the initiative to request land on the east side of the Jordan in the territories of the kingdoms of Sihon and Og, the Amorite kings that the Israelites had destroyed and wiped out on the east of the Jordan. The Transjordan tribes approached Moses and asked for that land to settle. That represented a reversal of the scheme that really should apply. The text indicates that it is up to God to decide who goes where and what tribe goes with what land. As we read in the book of Numbers, Moses was initially really put off by this. He was angered by it because it's not up to Israel to decide if they want to live in a particular place.

Also, Moses was concerned that these tribes would not help their kindred. They would simply settle down. But the situation resulted in an agreement in which Moses agreed that those tribes could have the lands east of the Jordan if they were willing to help their kindred fight to take their lands west of the Jordan. They agreed to do so. So, Joshua now reminds these tribes of their obligation.

Joshua's reminder establishes an occasion to present Israel as obedient and uniformly faithful to its obligations as set out by Moses. Their response to Joshua is emphatic. In a sense, we are prompted to see them speaking now for the entire nation. *They answered Joshua: 'All that you have commanded us we will do, and wherever you send us we will go. Just as we obeyed Moses in all things, so we will obey you. Only may the LORD your God be with you, as he was with Moses! Whoever rebels against your orders and disobeys your words, whatever you command, shall be put to death. Only be strong and courageous."* As the Transjordan affirm their obedience, devotion and complete compliance with Joshua, and the commands of Moses, they echo some of the Lord's language to Joshua in the initial speech.

So, the first chapter ends with an emphatic declaration of obedience on the part of the eastern tribes of Reuben, Gad and half Manasseh: "We are going to be completely obedient to the commands of Moses. Joshua, we are going to be completely obedient to you. Therefore, we are going to be wholly obedient to the Lord." There is complete unanimity.

When the story begins (cf. Numbers 32:1–42; Deuteronomy 3:12–22), there is an implicit division between these tribes who want territory east. Nevertheless, the latter of chapter one portrays complete unanimity with their kindred, and the entire nation is going to cross over together. Israel is wholeheartedly obedient. The Lord is with Joshua, and the Lord's words echo throughout this first chapter.

So, as chapter one concludes, the audience and readers are urged to remember Deuteronomy. They are prompted to think of what happens within the framework of Deuteronomy's theological perspective. The Lord is promising, the Lord is directing, and the Lord is giving assurance. At the same time, the nation is offering its complete, emphatic and unambiguous devotion and obedience.

LEADERSHIP PRINCIPLES

One crucial leadership principle that can be deduced from Joshua 1:1-18 is that those who occupy leadership positions in the local church do so under construction. Leaders fill their roles while having familial, educational and emotional deficiencies. While such deficiencies could hamper one's effectiveness in ministry if gone unattended over time, these deficiencies will inevitably arise at some point—as displayed in Joshua's inauguration speech as He is installed as Israel's new leader.

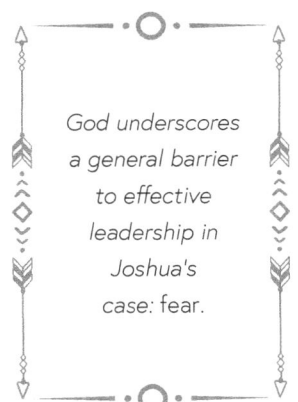

God underscores a general barrier to effective leadership in Joshua's case: fear.

God underscores a general barrier to effective leadership in Joshua's case: *fear*. Mentioned numerous times in the sections above, the repetitive motifs of courage and strength make it evident that fear was a stumbling block that could prevent Joshua, and all of Israel, from experiencing the fullness of God's blessing. The passage does not give details about the cause of Joshua's fear; thus, leaving room for the reader to infer.

Perhaps fear in Joshua welled as he: 1) reviewed the past; and 2) ruminated on the future. It is likely that as Joshua camped on the other side of the river, across from Israel's promise, he stared back into Israel's history and recalled the unique encounters Moses had with God. As a result, Joshua could have felt incompetent in comparison to Moses. It is also likely that Joshua's fear could have resulted in Joshua's awareness of the military prowess of his enemies. Whatever the cause of Joshua's fear might have been, God had stalled the advancement of His plan.

Historical Foundations

The essence of the Christian faith walk is a process of reconciliation that leads to restoration. Therefore, it is no surprise that restoration is a constant occurrence in the life of the Church. It is the reason for which parishioners gather each week. It is the opportunity to see someone restored to Christ through the gift of reconciliation. Thus, the Church of God—the Kingdom of God—is consistently being restored to right fellowship with the Father.

The members of Faith Church are likewise keenly aware of the effects of reconciliation and what that restoration has done for humanity. Since the members of Faith Church understand the necessity of such a reconciliation between God and man, they must also understand the necessity of reconciliation between one another. This is not simply about individualized reconciliation but examining the causes of communal reconciliation. It also means examining how that same reconciliation provides restoration to all who are willing to participate in the process of it. Through this brief historical view, an understanding of the historicity of communal restoration in antiquity to the present day is imperative to the potential experience for the members of Faith Church to encounter the same.

For hundreds of years, those within and outside of the Christian faith have long discussed the condition of humanity. Such a condition was not the intention of God as He desired and desires fellowship with His creation. From day to night, to the next day, and for six days, there was set in motion the creation of the Creator. Day and night in a harmonious relationship, nature in harmony with its Creator, then man in fellowship with God. As part of this fellowship, man is given access to the Garden of Eden.

There in the garden is the home of humanity to enjoy the presence of God forever. Eden is where the LORD God planted a garden in the east. There, he put the man whom he had formed. Out of the ground, the LORD God made to spring up every tree that is pleasant to the sight and good for food. The tree of life was in the midst of the garden, as well as the tree of the knowledge of good and evil. A river flowed out of Eden to water the garden, and there it divided and became four rivers.[56] Eden was the perfect place for humanity and for all of God's creation. It was a place of provision, a place of fellowship, and a place of happiness.

It is likewise in the book of Genesis where one not only learns of the creation of man, but the fall of man. This reality has been at the forefront of much conversation as it relates to the Christian experience. Those who choose the side of Adam would suggest that he was tricked by Eve, and thus, should essentially be seen as a victim of her actions. Those who choose the side of Eve suggest that Eve was tricked by the serpent and Adam, as the man or the head, could have chosen not to partake in the eating of the fruit. No matter where blame is placed—or not—the reality remains that sins sits at the heart of such an act. Satan's desire was to be equal with God. It is never the job of the creation to be equal to its Creator. It was impossible.

Where the need existed, God in turn created a plan for humanity.

Such a separation created the path for sin. Sin is what humanity has fallen into. This is the Genesis for the need of

---

[56] Gn 2:8-10 (ESV).

reconciliation. It has always been sin that caused humanity to attempt to go its own way—apart from God. Sin broke the heart of God as humanity refused to live according to the law God provided and the words He spoke. Generation after generation, the Bible details that sin permeated humanity. An entire flood was sent to wipe out those in humanity whom God was displeased with and to give those who remained the experience of His grace—to remain and have a fresh start. Yet, sin still maneuvered its way back in the midst of man. Despite the prophets who were raised up to communicate the importance of humanity's hearts turning back to God, for good, sin still permeated creation. Where the need existed, God in turn created a plan for humanity.

It is in Genesis 3:15 (ESV) that we learn of the proto-Evangelium of God. This is the first mentioning of the Gospel, or the "Good News." God says to the serpent, *"I will put enmity between you and the woman, and between your offspring and her offspring; he shall bruise your head and you shall bruise his heel."* Essentially, Satan, in the form of the serpent, has been the enemy of humanity since humanity's fall in the Garden of Eden. He has been, and will only be, allowed to continue in such a capacity until the time that God sends Christ to return. However, until then, humanity was in desperate need of divine intervention and assistance. It is here that God first articulates the reconciliation of humanity.

Therefore, reconciliation is the plan of God, not man. It has been the testimony of God to reconcile man back unto Himself. What is incredibly gracious is that God does not simply provide restoration for His chosen people. The Jews, His chosen people, are not the only beneficiaries of such a monumental act of grace. To the Jew and the Gentile, mercy and grace are given. It is a communal effort. It is an effort that sees the need for the *body* to be restored, not simply the *individual*.

What must be addressed is that communal restoration was necessary for humanity. God knew the effects of such an event in the Garden would have an eternal impact on humanity as a whole. This is the importance of understanding that Christianity does not happen in a vacuum. Neither does ministry. What one person does affects those around them, as well. Such an effect required communal reconciliation to be afforded to humanity. It was not enough for this reconciliation to be individualized. That one mistake, or sin in the Garden of Eden, changed the course of humanity forever.

In any case, the issue that is presented comes where man is separated from the presence of God. The underlying problem here is the great rift between God and humanity in the infinite qualitative difference between eternity and time. God is the eternal, merciful God who stands over sinful, time-bound humanity. Once again, the solution to this "againstness" of God toward humanity is found in the reconciling event of God in the third time-sphere, "God's time for us."[57] It is not simply a physical separation. Humanity's fall was so intense that it would take the sacrifice of Christ, the Father in the flesh, to rescue humanity from such a fate. It is the reconciliation humanity never knew it even needed.

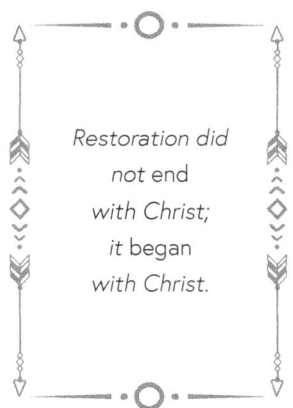

Restoration did not end with Christ; it began with Christ.

If the example of communal restoration and reconciliation through God are to be understood, it has to be understood through this lens. It must be viewed through the reconciliation and restoration that has come to humanity through the grace of God and the person of Jesus Christ. It is Christ who would be sent to be the mediator between God and man. This mediation would set the example for all of humanity. His example provides for man a model of restoration that is available in a top-down form: reconciliation and restoration from God to man, and from man to man. All of this is possible because of the grace of God through Jesus Christ.

---

[57] James J. Cassidy, *God's Time for Us: Barth's Reconciliation of Eternity and Time in Jesus Christ* (Bellingham, WA: Lexham Press, 2016), 62.

Restoration did not *end* with Christ; it *began* with Christ. The continuation of restoration is present in the Scriptures of antiquity, as well. One of the biggest influences in the New Testament church comes through the witness of the Apostle Paul. It is through Paul's experience with Christ where the restoration made available to him is extended, by him, to others throughout his ministry. This cannot be overlooked.

It is the Apostle Paul who has restoration experience as a result of being reconciled to Christ. Saul, as he was once known, was a persecutor of Christians. He was known for his deeds done against those who walked with Christ. It is not until Saul is questioned, directly by God while on the road to Damascus, that God calls out to him, *saying, "Saul, Saul, why are you persecuting me?"* And he said, *"Who are you, Lord?"* And he said, *"I am Jesus, whom you are persecuting"* (Acts 9:4-5, ESV). Blinded by the light from Heaven, which preceded the voice of God, Saul is guided, by hand, to Ananias, who would be the one to heal him.

His restoration is not done in isolation. Ironically, Saul is spiritually blind to the persecution he has brought on the disciples of the Lord. Saul is then blinded physically as his spiritual eyes are open to the truth of Jesus Christ. Because of this exchange, Saul's name is changed to Paul, and he must now depend on the faithfulness of another one of God's servants to be of help to him. Someone had to take

Paul to the home of Ananias, after he is blinded, and Ananias would be the one to lay his hands on Paul. The reluctance of Ananias to have anything to do with Saul, despite the Lord's instruction, highlights the metamorphosis of Saul from a truly fearsome persecutor. In significant harmony with Acts' previous stress on Christological belief, the new convert preaches that, "Jesus is the Son of God" (9:20).[58] With this act, Paul's vision is restored for the work of ministry, and he wastes no time after being restored.

It was not by accident that Saul would be reconciled to Christ and exposed to communal restoration. The very message of Christ emphasizes community in the plan of salvation for all of humanity. Saul's restoration happens in community with others. This is important to what will be known about Paul. This example and experience of communal restoration would be seen in the ministry of Paul throughout the New Testament. It would also set an example for others to practice communal restoration.

One way in which Paul emphasizes communal restoration, as seen in the New Testament after his own experience, is found in Colossians. The church at Colossae was written, by Paul, during his time in captivity. The issue Paul primarily

---

[58] Raymond E. Brown, *An Introduction to the New Testament* (New York, NY: Doubleday, 1997), 298.

addressed with the church was that of the false teachings and teachers who were present at the Colossian church. Those who sought to rewrite the story of Christ's work were seeking to change the perspective of those who belonged to the Colossian church. It was Paul's mission to communicate to them the dangers they found and would find themselves in if they embraced these false teachings.

Still, one additional emphasis comes in the form of the restoration of Onesimus. In his final greeting to them, Paul writes, *Tychicus will tell you all about my activities. He is a beloved brother and faithful minister and fellow servant in the Lord. I have sent him to you for this very purpose, that you may know how we are and that he may encourage your hearts, and with him Onesimus, our faithful and beloved brother, who is one of you. They will tell you of everything that has taken place here* (Colossians 4:7-9, ESV).

Onesimus is identified as the fugitive slave of Paul's friend Philemon. There are several perspectives on how Onesimus got to Paul. But the ultimate reality for Paul was that Onesimus was to be viewed as not a slave, but a brother. In fact, he is also mentioned in the book of Philemon as one who helped Paul. When Paul writes to the church, he essentially suggests to the church that they embrace and restore Onesimus. Paul requests that this work happens in the midst of the Colossian church. The restoration that

Onesimus would need would be amongst a community of individuals. It is a communal restoration that Paul suggests to the church on behalf of Onesimus.

It is clear that the church at Thessalonica was indeed one of Paul's beloved churches of the New Testament. Still, there were congregational matters that Paul would address in his letter to them. Even as believers are to be appreciative of and responsive to congregational leaders, they are

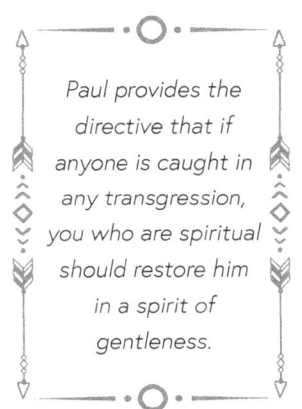

Paul provides the directive that if anyone is caught in any transgression, you who are spiritual should restore him in a spirit of gentleness.

also to be committed to each other's well-being (5:14-15). They are to warn the unruly, "encourage the disheartened, help the weak be patient with everyone" (5:14). Far from marginalizing and ignoring those with needs among them, they are to be one another's keeps. Forgoing retaliation ("pay[ing] back wrong for wrong"), they are to pursue, "what is good for each other and for everyone else" (5:15).[59]

For Paul, the work at the church in Thessalonica was not a ministry of isolation and individualism. If the church would work to restore its brother, it would have to be done in community with others. With relevance to Galatians 6,

---

[59] Bruce W. Longnecker and Todd D. Still, *Thinking Through Paul* (Grand Rapids, MI: Zondervan, 2014), 73.

Paul essentially suggests that it is the job of those who are spiritual to act in communal restoration of their brothers. Paul provides the directive that if anyone is caught in any transgression, you who are spiritual should restore him in a spirit of gentleness. Keep watch on yourself, lest you too be tempted (Galatians 6:1, ESV). He suggests that it is a community effort to restore a brother or sister who may have fallen in their faith.

This same emphasis of communal restoration would also be seen in the work of the church at Philippi. Paul's relationship with the Philippian church is mostly known as one that he long loved. It is obvious that the Philippian church would have been Paul's most beloved church. This can be seen and understood through the contents of his letter to them thanking them for their faithfulness to the work of the ministry and even their financial support to his work in ministry.

What Paul also emphasizes, in the vein of communal restoration, is the restoration of unity within the Philippian church. Yes, the church at Philippi was Paul's most beloved. But they also had various issues that called for restoration amongst them. Paul exhorts the Philippians to follow Jesus' example of humility and obedience to God's will. Following Jesus' example will help the congregation maintain unity and faithfulness (2:1-4,12-18, 4:2-3).[60] Paul suggests to the congregation that if there is any encouragement in Christ, any comfort from love, any participation in the Spirit, any affection and sympathy, complete my joy by being of the same mind, having the same love, being in full accord and of one mind (Philippians 2:1-2, ESV). This is an appropriate admonition from Paul as chapter four of this same epistle would provide brief details about the situation between Euodia and Syntyche.

According to the letter, there is a measure of disagreement between the two women. Some scholars suggest that the two women were not at odds with one another. It is suggested that Euodia and Syntyche are not arguing but are being gently reminded of the grace of humility, as well as the importance of unity. It is also suggested that the yokefellow is not an individual, but an apostrophe for the Philippian congregation; the congregation is simply being asked to cooperate with Euodia and Syntyche.[61] Whether the issue between Euodia and Syntyche is seen as them being at odds with one another or not, it is clear that there was a need for the restoration of unity between the two as an example to the Philippian church.

---

[60] Andrew E. Arterbury, W. H. Bellinger, Jr, and Derek S. Dodson, *Engaging Christian Scriptures* (Grand Rapids, MI: Baker Academic, 2014), 224.

[61] Richard G Fellows and Alistair C Stewart. "Euodia, Syntyche and the Role of Syzygos: Phil 4:2–3." *Zeitschrift für die Neutestamentliche Wissenschaft und die Kunde der älteren Kirche* 109, no. 2 (2018): 222–234.

What Paul highlights is that in order to achieve the unity that he is calling for amongst all members of the Philippian church—and really the entire body of Christ--he asserts that these types of issues must not be ignored. His solution to resolving these issues and others, according to him, is to bring them to the forefront and discuss them in a way beneficial to the Kingdom of God. It is also imperative to understand that this issue existed within the congregation of his most beloved church. Essentially, these were some of Paul's most faithful parishioners and even they needed a measure of restoration amongst them.

As a contrast of congregations, the Corinthian church was a congregation that came with many of its own issues. As Paul opens his letter to the Corinthians in 1 Corinthians, after greeting them, he immediately addresses the factions and disturbances amongst this church. Paul makes an appeal to them that they all agree, and that there be no divisions among them, but that they be united in the same mind and the same judgment (1 Corinthians 1:10, ESV). Paul has gotten word that there are several issues that exist in the congregation, and they need to be restored to unity if they are to continue the work of Christ.

Paul, in 2 Corinthians 2, expresses his sorrow as it relates to his visit with the church. In response to Paul's "tearful" letter, the Corinthians have disciplined this person. But now,

Paul urges mercy and forgiveness. Paul tells the Corinthians that he wants to heal his relationship with them.[62] The individual that the Corinthian church has decided to discipline is known to Paul. He calls for them to restore the individual and themselves through acts of mercy and forgiveness. The truth was that it was not simply the individual who needed to be restored. The church of Corinth, too, stood in need of restoration. To this point, Paul desired restoration between him and the church of Corinth.

Beyond the antiquity of the New Testament epistles, there was also a need for communal restoration amongst the macro movements of church history. One of the primary avenues of restoration came in the 16th century as frustration with the Catholic church continued to rise. At the heart of the issues with the Catholic Church stood the issue of indulgences and what it meant for the believer's justification. For the Catholic church, there was a spiritual necessity and an economic benefit for the system of indulgences that existed. While the system taught that individuals could be absolved of their transgressions, it also built a very tangible and healthy system of wealth for the Catholic church. This seemed to become the motivation for such a system of justification that would eventually be confronted.

---

[62] Brown, *An Introduction to the New Testament*, 544.

For many who were connected to the Catholic church, this was a broken system. It was a system that did not wholeheartedly concern itself with the souls of the people it served, but it sought to ensure that its own financial health was taken care of. There were several who were disturbed by such a system and began to raise concerns for what was happening in the Catholic church. It would be Martin Luther who would take a macro approach to reformation. Luther's opposition to the system that stood in place was risky but proved to change the course of the church.

Luther was in torment, almost to the point of desperation and resentment toward God, because all his religious and penitential observances did not succeed in making him feel accepted by God nor at peace with God. What transformed this inner experience into a real religious chain reaction was the issue of indulgences, which made Luther decide to send his famous ninety-five theses to Archbishop Albrecht von Magdeburg and to the doctors of the University on October 31, 1517.[63] What Luther primarily opposed was the tradition of Catholicism as it related to justification. They believed that justification began with baptism and would continue with works. Luther fought against this because the system was being abused by the church. The Protestant

---

[63] Raniero Cantalamessa, "'The Righteousness of God Has Been Manifested': The Fifth Centenary of the Protestant Reformation, an Occasion of Grace and Reconciliation for the Whole Church," *Journal of ecumenical studies* 53, no. 3 (2018): 423–435.

movement provoked a reaction from the church of Rome, which decided it needed to do two things: rid itself of the worst abuses and corruptions that had led some princes of the Holy Roman Empire to support the Protestants; and firm up its own theology by deciding and declaring once and for all what Christian truth would be regarding Scripture and tradition, salvation and the church.[64]

Luther's decision fought back against a system set up by the Catholic church and sought to restore the faith of believers near and far. Many saw Luther's act as an aggressive approach to articulating his issue with the church. However, it was actually a reflection of what the Apostle Paul suggested: to bring an issue to the forefront and not allow it to linger too long. If restoration were to come to the Western Church, Luther thought it imperative to have a theology that created an emphasis around justification by faith alone. This was the restoration he sought for the church. This was the restoration the church desperately needed during this time in history. Still, Luther's post of the ninety-five theses was not simply a posting of antiquity without purpose and explanation.

He would certainly spend his days teaching and preaching the theology of justification by faith. What he also did was

---

[64] Roger E. Olson, *The Story of Christian Theology* (Downers Grove, IL: InterVarsity Press, 1999), 371.

take advantage of the printing press to spread the message of justification by faith alone. He sought to ensure that the information could be provided beyond the door of the Wittenburg church. In the process, Luther created what was essentially a new form of theological writing: lucid, accessible and, above all, short.[65] He realized that the restoration that was sought could happen in communities, small and large, and provided the information for such a theology to be taught.

As a result, the Western church essentially divides and is reformed. The Western church would eventually see variations of Luther's theology. There were theologians like Ulrich Zwingli, John Calvin, those associated with the Church of England and even the Anabaptist who would have their take on the reformation movement. In particular, Zwingli would become a mentee of Luther during his lifetime. Many nineteenth-century historians of the reformation were fascinated by comparisons of the two men in thought and character, often finding in Luther the mystical monk and, in Zwingli, the social, communal reformer. Indisputably, the Wittenberger has remained the pre-eminent figure in the triumphal narrative of Protestantism's victory over a corrupt medieval Church. Zwingli was at best Batman's Robin. At worst, the Joker.[66]

---

[65] Andrew Pettegree, *Brand Luther* (New York, NY: Penguin Books, 2015), 62.

[66] Bruce F Gordon, *Zwingli: God's Armed Prophet* (New Haven, CT: Yale University Press, 2021), 164.

Still, Zwingli would develop his own lens of theology that mostly agreed with Luther's, but with a variation based on his own conviction. Even others influenced by Martin Luther's boldness to challenge the system of the Catholic church, as it related to communicating justification to parishioners, were greatly influenced by Luther's convictions—even if they had variations to it. Many of those after Luther agreed that justification was by faith alone or imputed, but they had variations on baptism, communion, church and state, or even human will. The ultimate point is that even in the variation, the restoration that was needed came to the Church.

Their work opened the world up to the varying Christian traditions today. Although it was certainly a risky approach, what Martin Luther did to challenge the Catholic church has helped shape the faith of millions of people today. What he taught was that the Bible, not the Catholic Church, was the central authority of the faith. One could suppose that Luther's work restored faith within the faith. It was a transformational movement that opened the eyes of many to the nature of God. This is not to say that Luther provided a totally perfect perspective of faith. Still, it is to say that the contributions he did make opened the door for more understanding within Christianity. Because the Catholic church seemingly determined who was pardoned and who was not, the work that Luther did also restored the sacrament to the Church. It was no longer up to the Catholic church who would be able to receive it based on a system of indulgences. Luther set a standard that would offer sacrament to all who believed in Christ, with no need for payment to the church.

The more micro of movements, in comparison of the present day, have a history of, and still stand in need of, reconciliation and restoration. One denominational movement that was and is in desperate need of reconciliation that could provide restoration to the church at large would be under the Southern Baptist Convention. The year 1814 marked the beginning of an era for Baptists; 1845 marked its end. Baptists who had tried to unite the denomination saw it succumb to schism. Whatever official names they have used, Baptists, since 1845, have required some regional prefix; they were no longer just "Baptists"; but "Northern" and "Southern" Baptists.[67] The Great Schism of 1845 was the breakdown of a general Baptist system in America. This schism came to be because of those who would speak out against the evils of slavery within the Baptist tradition.

Several leaders of the Baptist tradition, in America, opposed slavery. They were essentially Northern Baptist. The result of this opposition is that Northern Baptist and

---

[67] H. Leon McBeth, *The Baptist Heritage* (Nashville, TN: Broadman Press, 1987), 391.

Southern Baptist organizations were formed. This 19th century reality in the south became a stain for the Southern Baptist Convention as it moved into the 20th century. As race relations continue to rise, the Southern Baptist Convention eventually atoned for such a history—at least in a way that at the moment did not seem as performative then as it may be communicated now. In 1995, the convention would issue a formal apology for its involvement in the evils of slavery. This was the start of the restoration needed for Southern Baptists.

This restoration was necessary because the foundation of such an entity was based on the opportunity to enslave Black people. If Southern Baptists sought to truly atone for what was a very distinct part of their history, they had to make moves that "proved" they were ready for a measure of reconciliation. One of those measures came in the form of Dr. Fred Luter, Jr. A native of Louisiana, Dr. Luter would become the first African American president of the Southern Baptist Convention in 2012. The denomination also offered alternative names for those member congregations who did not want to be associated with the dark past of slavery and the Southern Baptist Convention.

The Presbyterian tradition would also have its issues regarding slavery and the Southern Baptist Convention would not be the only denomination to renounce slavery.

In the minutes of the 1793 assembly, the members of the Presbyterian denomination reconciled that the Assembly observed that although in some sections of the country, under certain circumstances, the transfer of slaves may be unavoidable; yet, they consider the buying and selling of slaves by way of traffic, and all undue severity in the management of them, as inconsistent with the spirit of the Gospel. They recommended it to the Presbyteries and Sessions…to make use of all prudent measures to prevent such shameful and unrighteous conduct.[68] It was clear that this was the commencement of racial reconciliation. Even though the Presbyterian denomination, as well as the Southern Baptist Denomination, had much more work to do in order for racial reconciliation to reach its full potential within their sphere, this was the start that was necessary for them.

Denouncing slavery, what was once lawfully a right to Whites in America, was the restoration that was necessary to the humanity of Blacks in America and across the world. Methodists would not be estranged from this means of racial reconciliation either. This denomination, too, would have to atone for its involvement in slavery. The Methodist church would also issue a formal apology for its hand in slavery. This was only the start of restoration for Blacks in America.

---

[68] *Man-Stealing and Slavery Denounced by the Presbyterian and Methodist Churches: Together with an Address to All the Churches*, (n.p. Boston, MA, 1834).

Still, some of this "progress" seems to have regressed with a new issue on the table. The Southern Baptist Convention is one of the leading organizations who are against the teaching and communication of CRT, or Critical Race Theory. Many Southern Baptist leaders and churches have adamantly articulated their opposition to the teachings or communication of CRT. This is clearly still an area that stands to have reconciliation within this denomination. What is interesting is that many oppose it and there are others within the denomination that are open to the conversation of CRT, and even ascribe to it as members of the Southern Baptist Convention (SBC). This issue has also caused another schism within the SBC as several churches once affiliated with the SBC have decided to cease their alignment with the convention.

What is even more damaging to the convention and another hot issue on the table is the latest report of moral failure and physical abuses within the Southern Baptist Convention. A 2022 report on the conventions' members' indiscretions and infidelity between pastor of the Southern Baptist Convention and their victims is the newest need for restoration in the denomination. The Southern Baptist Convention sex abuse report rocked the denomination as the report has been released and the names of the accusers are to follow. The nearly 300-page report included confidential emails and memos between longtime lawyers for the 13-million-member denomination and leaders of the Southern Baptist Convention's administrative arm. The report details top leaders repeatedly tried to bury sex abuse claims and lied about what they could do, a former SBC president was considered "credibly accused" of sexual

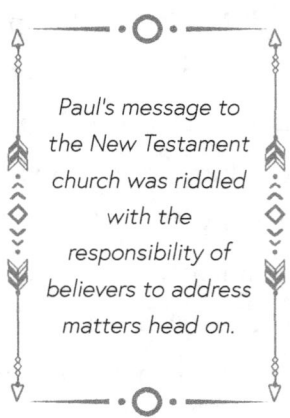

Paul's message to the New Testament church was riddled with the responsibility of believers to address matters head on.

assault, unheeded warnings went on for decades, and leaders seemed to put concern over potential litigation over people's safety.[69]

There is clearly restoration needed within the Southern Baptist denomination. The parishioners' faith has been rocked as a result of the moral failures that currently exist in the leadership. Reconciliation and restoration will only be able to be achieved when the truth is made public, and measures of atonement are put in place for those who have sinned against others.

What is apparent is that the Southern Baptist Convention has not taken the accountability and the responsibility, as a whole, to address the inconsistencies and indecencies of

---

[69] Emily McFarlan Miller, "After Years of Debate, Conservatives Split from the United Methodist Church," *The Washington Post*, last modified May 6, 2022, accessed September 14, 2022, https://www. washingtonpost.com/religion/2022/05/06/after-years-loud-debate-conservatives-quietly-split-united-methodist-church/.

its leaders within the denomination. Paul's message to the New Testament church was riddled with the responsibility of believers to address matters head on. Perhaps Paul's admonishment was not only for the sake of being in right fellowship with Christ, but also a need to be in right fellowship with man—brother/sister to brother/sister. It cannot be dismissed that the Southern Baptist Convention's refusal to handle each issue as it arose has created the firestorm that is the 2022 sexual abuse report of the denomination.

It is likewise shocking that the denomination would seek atonement for their involvement in slavery, yet still essentially issue abuse to its Black members as it refuses to accept, as a whole, the reality of Critical Race Theory and how the theory is proven within the denomination itself. Being aware of the reality that there are effects of slavery that exist because many of their members supported, and still support, the enslavement of Blacks is what Critical Race Theory is calling for—in addition to non-performative atonement. It is the necessity of understanding the legacy of the enslavement of Blacks in America, and across the world. Still, the Southern Baptist Convention does not currently desire to reconcile through this medium of discussion.

The Southern Baptist Convention is not the only denomination that needs restoration. The United Methodist

Church has experienced a recent schism that has split their denomination, as well. The year 2022 would not be the start of these issues within the United Methodist Church. In a 2014 article, it was recognized that a split was possible. The UMC's governing document, the Book of Discipline, calls clergy into a "covenant of mutual care and accountability." This document had been amended to state that clergy who perform same-sex weddings are guilty of a "chargeable offense." A growing number of UMC clergy began performing such ceremonies in open defiance of the Book of Discipline, prompting a series of church trials, which bitterly divided the church. John Komperis, United Methodist director for the Institute on Religion and Democracy, added that one former minister "was not the first United Methodist minister to be defrocked for crossing these lines and would not be the last."[70]

This was only a preview of coming attractions for the United Methodist Church as the denomination would see a huge effect of such mandates. Today's opposition to same-sex marriages, and ordination of gay clergy, became a huge issue in the denomination. It is a battle between conservative United Methodist Church members and more liberal members of the United Methodist Church. After decades of rancorous debate over the ordination and

---

[70] Amy Frykholm, "A Time to Split?" *The Christian Century (1902)* 131, no. 8 (2014): 22.

marriage of LGBTQ United Methodists, a special session of the United Methodist Church's General Conference, and three postponements of a vote to formally split the denomination, the schism finally came "without fanfare, but full of hope, faith, and perseverance." There is also the launch of the Global Methodist Church, a new theologically conservative denomination splintering from the United Methodist Church.[71] Such a transition within the denomination has created a need for reconciliation. A history of splits, not simply in the United Methodist tradition, but in all traditions, is a cry for reconciliation.

This history of communal reconciliation and restoration that happened in antiquity, and which still needs to happen in the present day of the Church, is necessary and ongoing. There is a chronology of reconciliation and restoration that exists and has set the example for the Church today. The story and reality of reconciliation and restoration began with the work of God through Jesus Christ. Humanity was in desperate need of fellowship with God where sin separated God the Creator from His creation. Still beyond the failure and fall of humanity, God chose to reconcile humanity to Himself. It took the sacrifice of Christ to offer salvation that could restore the fellowship between God and man.

---

[71] Miller, "After Years of Debate."

Where the example of Christ was witnessed by those who believed in His messianic presence, and seen by those who opposed it, the example of restoration and reconciliation became a part of the witness of the New Testament Church. Not limited to the ministry of Paul, it is his epistles that provide insight as to how humanity could take on the nature of Christ, through the Holy Spirit, to offer reconciliation and restoration between one another and in a broader community of believers. For Paul, reconciliation and restoration were not just words to articulate; it was a standard to live by. It was expressed through the actions of the believer. Perhaps Paul may not have known the extent to which his letters would reach, but certainly he recognized that the churches he wrote to would be able to read and hear about his experiences and the teachings he was making available to them. Where they were willing to be instructed, the Word of God could come alive to them.

The simple promises of change are not enough to bring the restoration needed.

This chronology continues in the macro historical movements and the micro (denominational) historical movements, as well. Within those movements, it is clear that where some areas of reconciliation or restoration have begun, there begs another call to the same as certain conversations continue and certain details are continuously exposed. Martin Luther would not be the only person to challenge an existing macro system of Christianity, but it was likewise seen in the Wesley brothers' opposition to the Church of England. John and Charles Wesley believed that a measure of restoration was needed in their time, and they chose the Methodist movement as the medium of change and restoration.

The simple promises of change are not enough to bring the restoration needed. Performative acts of atonement are not going to create the change that is so desperately needed in any church sphere. What is clear is that having a history of what reconciliation and restoration can look like, and should look like, is a great foundation to the Church of today being a part of such a task. It is the task of being a part of the work of the Kingdom of God to help restore humanity. Where the Church is able to properly address issues as they arise within the Church, it is possible that communal reconciliation and restoration can happen. This is also a reality for which Faith Church can participate and eventually implement for others.

HISTORICAL SUCCESSION

Rome claims that its teachings are true because it possesses the Apostolic succession of office, wherein its bishops follow one after another from the Apostles. Furthermore, the apostles promised apostolic succession in the office of the bishop to guarantee truth. On the other hand, Protestants say that we are right because we have the apostolic succession of teaching, not of office. It is the apostles' teachings that guarantee the truth, not the apostolic office. The apostles never taught the apostolic succession of offices. They did, however, teach the apostolic succession of truth, which was to be preserved in the Scriptures for us always. So, we believe in the apostolic succession—not of office—but of truth.[72]

The Apostles and Apostolic Succession in History

The documents of the New Testament show that in the early days of the Church, and in the lifetime of the apostles,

---

[72] "What is Apostolic Succession," *Ligonier Ministries*, accessed August 8, 2022, https://www. ligonier.org/learn/qas/what-is-apostolic-succession.

there was diversity in the way communities were organized. Also, in the period immediately following, there was a tendency to assert and strengthen the ministry of teaching and leadership. Those who directed communities in the lifetime of the apostles, or after their death, have different names in the New Testament texts: the presbyteroi-episkopoi are described as poimenes, hegoumenoi, proistamenoi, kyberneseis. In comparison with the rest of the Church, the feature of the presbyteroi-episkopoi is their apostolic ministry of teaching and governing. Whatever the method by which they are chosen whether through the authority of The Twelve or Paul, or some link with them, they share in the authority of the apostles who were instituted by Christ and who maintain for all time their unique character.[73]

In the course of time, this ministry underwent a development. This development happened by internal necessity. It was encouraged by external factors, and above all, by the need to maintain unity in communities and to defend them against errors. When communities were deprived of the actual presence of apostles, and yet still wanted to refer to the authority, there had to be some way of continuing to exercise adequately the functions that the

---

[73] "Catholic Teaching on Apostolic Succession," *International Theology Commission*, accessed August 8, 2022, https://www.vatican.va/roman_curia/congregations/cfaith/cti_documents/rc_cti_1973_successione-apostolica_en.html.

apostles had exercised in and in relation to them. Already in the New Testament texts, there are echoes of the transition from the apostolic period to the subapostolic age, and one begins to see signs of the development that in the second century led to the stabilization and general recognition of the episcopal ministry. The stages of this development can be glimpsed in the last writings of the Pauline Tradition and in other texts linked with the authority of the apostles.[74]

The significance of the apostles at the time of the foundation of the earliest Christian communities was held to be essential for the structure of the Church and local communities in the thinking of the subapostolic period. The principle of the apostolicity of the Church elaborated in this reflection led to the recognition of the ministry of teaching and governing as an institution derived from Christ by and through the mediation of the apostles. The Church lived in the certain conviction that Jesus, before He left this world, sent The Twelve on a universal mission and promised that He would be with them at all times until the end of the world (Matthew 28:18-20).[75]

As one can see from the New Testament writings, conflicts could not always be avoided between individuals and communities and the authority of the ministry. Paul, on the

---

[74] "Catholic Teaching on Apostolic Succession."

[75] Ibid.

one hand, strove to understand the Gospel with and in the community and so to work out with them norms for Christian life. But, on the other hand, he appealed to his apostolic authority whenever it was a matter of the truth of the Gospel (see Galatians) or unyielding principles of Christian life (see 1 Corinthians 7). Likewise, the ministry of governing should never be separated from the community in such a way as to place itself above it. Its role is one of service in and for the community. But when the New Testament communities accept apostolic government, whether from the apostles themselves or their successors, then they obey and relate the authority of the ministry to that of Christ himself.[76]

During the second century, and after the Letter of Clement, this institution is explicitly acknowledged to carry with it the apostolic succession. Ordination with imposition of hands, already witnessed to in the pastoral epistles, appears in the process of clarification to be an important step in preserving the apostolic tradition and guaranteeing succession in the ministry. The documents of the third century (Tradition of Hippolytus) show that this conviction was arrived at peacefully and was considered to be a necessary institution. Clement and Irenaeus developed a doctrine on pastoral government and on the word in which

---

[76] Ibid.

they derive the idea of apostolic succession from the unity of the word, the unity of the mission, and the unity of the ministry of the Church; thus, apostolic succession became the permanent ground from which the Catholic Church understood its own nature.[77]

Apostolic Succession and Protestantism

When the Reformation took place, the doctrine of Apostolic Succession was not continued along with other doctrines. However, when you say, "Through church history, this doctrine [apostolic succession] seems to be strongly affirmed," you would be correct. It certainly has been accepted and defended for a long time by the Roman Catholic Church. You would also be correct in saying that, "When the Reformation took place, this doctrine was not continued along with other doctrines."[78] The answer is that the Reformation recovered the pure teaching of the original apostles themselves. They never taught any such doctrine. If you read your New Testament carefully, you will see that the apostles were marked by several distinctive features like:

1. They were chosen by Christ himself in an immediate way, not through the instrumentality of others.

---

[77] Ibid.

[78] "Apostolic Church and Protestantism," *The Orthodox Presbybterian Church,* accessed August 8, 2009, https://opc.org/q1.html?question_id=341.

2. They were able to truthfully say that they had seen Jesus after He rose from the dead. Paul said: "Then last of all He was seen by me also, as by one born out of due time" (1 Corinthians 15:8). The fact that Paul was the last one who could say such a thing in the history of the world shows clearly that there can be no genuine apostolic succession.

3. They were endowed with supernatural powers that other men did not (and do not) have. They even raised physically dead people to life. Paul said: "The signs of a true apostle were performed among you with utmost patience, with signs and wonders and mighty works" (2 Corinthians 12:12).

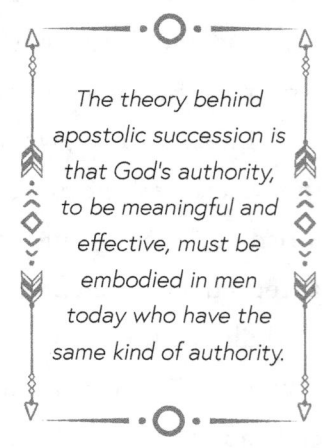

The theory behind apostolic succession is that God's authority, to be meaningful and effective, must be embodied in men today who have the same kind of authority.

4. They were qualified to speak with absolute and infallible authority. Paul could say in truth: "If anyone thinks himself to be a prophet or spiritual, let him acknowledge that the things which I write to you are the commandments of the Lord." No other individuals, other than the inspired prophets and apostles, could make statements like that. That is why

the things they said were by the plan and will of God preserved for us in the New Testament.[79]

The theory behind apostolic succession is that God's authority, to be meaningful and effective, must be embodied in men today who have the same kind of authority. But if you read carefully the following passage, you will see that this is not true at all.

In 1 Corinthians 5, Paul—who was not physically present in Corinth—wrote to them to tell them what to do with respect to a discipline case. He said (in 5:4-5): "In the name of our Lord Jesus Christ, when you are gathered together, along with my spirit, with the power of our Lord Jesus Christ, deliver such a one to Satan for the destruction of the flesh, that his spirit may be saved in the day of the Lord Jesus." So, you see, Paul did not pass on his authority to another man so that he could be there in Corinth. No, Paul said, in effect, if you will do what I as an apostle now instruct you to do, then I will be with you in spirit, and you will also have the power of our Lord Jesus with you, to deliver that man to Satan, etc.

---

[79] "Apostolic Church and Protestantism."

So, to put it simply, the Reformers realized there was no need for apostolic successors. No, the need was simply to have the apostles themselves with us through their inspired and inerrant teaching. That is what we have in the New Testament. The apostles never wrote anything that ever has needed, or ever will need, correction because they were inspired by God. Surely a person of average intelligence should be able to see that this has never been true of other men in history, no matter how strongly they may have believed themselves to be apostolic successors.[80]

Hope in the Face of Chronic Pain and Mortality

Hope is understood as living expectantly, ordinarily with specific hopes, even though the quality of expectancy is not reducible to particular expectations. Pain is the number one reason for visits to doctors. The American Medical Association has stated that pain in the United States is of endemic proportions. The most frequent cause of disability is arthritis. What if the pain stemming from such a "silent epidemic" were to become a normal expectation for a significant portion of the life span of most persons?[81]

---

[80] "Apostolic Church and Protestantism."

[81] Ralph L. Underwood, "Hope in the Face of Chronic Pain and Mortality," *Pastoral Psychology* 58 (5/6): 655–65, 2009, accessed August 5, 2022, doi:10.1007/s11089-009-0249-z.

Physical pain demands sufferers' attention. When the pain becomes unrelenting over time, it affects personal spirit, expectations, beliefs and hopes. Such pain has the capacity to alter personal identity and one's sense of meaning in life, to transform images of self and personal images of God. Interpretations and beliefs about pain range from pain as punishment to pain as salvation. The significance and meaning that people ascribe to their pain definitely affects how they experience pain and how they manage it. Pain researchers have examined so-called "premorbid" habits of mind, such as catastrophizing and ruminating as virtually toxic in the way they intensify pain in some persons' lives. On the other hand, realistic optimism contributes greatly to a person's readiness to cope with pain. Lest one unwittingly "blame the victim" or promote self-righteousness, it is important to note that such mental processes are acquired in a wide variety of ways.[82]

The Sufferings Are Better

According to Martin Luther, every action undertaken by man's initiative, and in his nature, is necessarily rebellion against God. This pervasive corruption adhered to man's mental and intellectual actions as much as to his emotional and physical movements. As Luther later would make more explicit, all of man's intellectual endeavors, even man's

---

[82] Underwood, "Hope in the Face of Chronic Pain and Mortality," 655.

attempt to know and understand God through His general revelation, were pervaded by arrogance and pride and, thus, were unacceptable in God's sight. For Luther, there was a moral component even to man's thinking and knowing; thus, such intellectual activities were disfigured by his sinful nature. Simply stated, man cannot rely on his reason to help him understand the infinite and holy God.[83]

While Luther openly espoused these revolutionary ideas in September 1517, he did not attract the Roman Catholic Church's attention until a month later when he posted his Ninety-Five Theses. The theses that Luther presented— twenty-eight theses dealing with theological matters and twelve dealing with philosophical matters—are known as *The Heidelberg Disputation.* They constitute perhaps the earliest crystallization of Luther's theology of the cross.[84] The starting point for Luther's theology of the cross is precisely what he posited in the Disputation Against Scholastic Theology: the moral limitations of man's natural knowledge of God. Luther was keenly aware of the pervasive and destructive arrogance of humanity, an arrogance that defiled even the operation of intellect.[85]

---

[83] Stephen G. Myers, "'The Sufferings Are Better': Martin Luther and the Theology of the Cross," *Puritan Reformed Journal* 9 (1): 84–100 201, accessed August 5, 2022, https://search-ebscohostcom.wilber forcepayne.idm.oclc.org/login.aspx?direct=true&db=rlh&AN=120832249&site=ehost-live.

[84] Myers, "The Sufferings Are Better," 87.

[85] Ibid, 88.

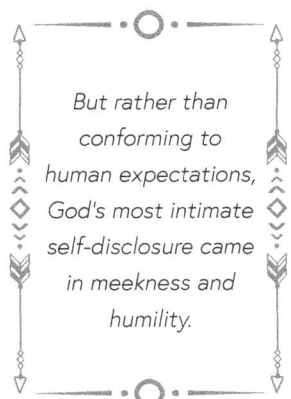

But rather than conforming to human expectations, God's most intimate self-disclosure came in meekness and humility.

Luther goes on to say that God does not reveal Himself and He does not accomplish redemption in a way that validates the arrogance of the strong and of the wise. Rather, God reveals Himself and He wins redemption with a humility that appears weak to the strong and foolish to the wise. Man would expect the sovereign Lord to disclose Himself in palpable strength and overwhelming glory. But rather than conforming to human expectations, God's most intimate self-disclosure came in meekness and humility.[86]

In short, then, the theology of the cross cuts to the heart of theological epistemology. How do we know what we know about God? Is our understanding of Him dictated by our own reason and expectations? Or is our understanding of God shaped by how He has revealed Himself both in His Word and pre-eminently on the cross? Does our human reasoning cause us to recoil from the "alien work" of God? Or does faith, leaning on God's revelation, enable us to see in the squalor of the alien work the silhouette of the sublime proper work? God has revealed Himself in humility and weakness, and coming to terms with that revelation is the necessary starting point of all true theology.[87]

---

[86] Ibid, 89.

[87] Myers, "The Sufferings Are Better," 93.

Human Suffering in Black Theology

The suffering of humanity is a theme that often seems to feature in speculation about whether or not God exists. The argument usually goes something like, "If God exists, why does God allow so much suffering?" The existence of both physical and mental suffering caused by illness, death, grief, poverty, famine, war, natural disasters and so forth is seen by some as confirmation that the existence of a deity is impossible, unlikely or, at the very least, pointless. Even for those with an existing faith, it can be a divisive issue. The personal experience or witnessing of suffering can cause some to draw closer to God as a source of strength and comfort. For others, this same suffering can be the very thing that causes them to lose their faith completely.[88]

In his work, *God of the Oppressed*, Cone devotes a chapter to the issue of suffering. He begins with acknowledging the challenging nature of a system that encompasses both the existence of suffering and a God who liberates the oppressed. However, Cone chooses not to tussle with the dilemma by turning to speculation that God is either not powerful enough or does not wish to end suffering. To choose either of these options is, according to Cone, "a violation of Black faith." He uses the Bible as his starting

---

[88] C. Troupes, "Human Suffering in Black Theology, *Black Theology: An International Journal*, 9(2), 199–222, 2011, accessed August 5, 2022, https://doi-org.wilberforcepayne.idm.oclc.org/10.1558/ blth. v9i2.199.

point for examining the issue of suffering. Here, he sees the dilemma reflected in the concrete existence of the people of Israel who, while believing in a faithful, loving and liberating God, nevertheless continued to experience suffering. Cone, working through the Old Testament, finds various explanations for the suffering of Israel: suffering as a test of faith, suffering as redemptive and suffering as part of the role of those who are chosen by God to struggle for the liberation of all humanity. Israel is cast as God's "Suffering Servant."[89]

Cone continues his exploration by looking at the New Testament, where Jesus takes over the role of Suffering Servant; his life and crucifixion are, for Cone, all illustrations of God entering into human suffering. "The cross of Jesus reveals the extent of God's involvement in the suffering of the weak. He is not merely sympathetic with the social pain of the poor but becomes totally identified with them in their agony and pain."[90] Jesus is the ever-present proof of God's liberating activity in the lives of the oppressed.

A Post-Holocaust Theology of Suffering

Sufferers facing trauma often experience an intense aloneness and feel spiritually deserted. The Holocaust

---

[89] Troupes, "Human Suffering in Black Theology," 201.

[90] Ibid.

provides the fiercest arena to pose the question of relationship with God in times of loss because it can be called the "ultimate abandonment." The very term "Holocaust" is derived from the Greek word holokauston, which means a sacrifice consumed by fire or "burnt whole." One of the far-reaching consequences of the Holocaust was that now a whole culture was forced to grapple with the fact that science and technology, the twin idols of modernity, produced state-of-the-art death camps. What remained was the truth that the humanistic celebration of independence from God and nature at its very core sustained an unprecedented capacity for death and demonic evil; therefore, the unique catastrophe of the Holocaust did not just impact the Jewish people, but it was a pivotal feature of the Twentieth century and a defining force in theological studies. The Nazis endeavored to eliminate, not only the Jews, but also the last vestiges of the fear and awe of God from the human conscience.[91]

There are many images of the suffering of God in the Old Testament that cannot be dismissed as attributions of human emotions. In the Scriptures, God expresses the pain of relationship with humanity through the metaphors of an

---

[91] Katherine A. Snyder, "A Post-Holocaust Theology of Suffering and Spiritual Grieving: Staying Attached to God in Loss," *Journal of Pastoral Counseling* 43 (November): 67–78, 2008, accessed August 5, 2022, https://search-ebscohost-com.wilberforcepayne.idm.oclc.org/login.aspx?direct=true&db=rlh&AN=46991875&site=ehost-live.

unproductive vineyard (Isaiah 5:1-10), a lost child (Luke 15: 11-32), and an adulterous wife (Hosea 3:1). These are all images of loss. Grieving begins with God. Encountering God-as-mystery can be enveloped in sorrow, but it is transformative when the suffocating box in which we have enclosed God, and our truest selves, is broken like Mary's alabaster jar (Matthew 26.6).

Justice without forgiveness cannot produce reconciliation.

Justice, Forgiveness and Reconciliation

This article explores what is regarded as three essential elements in atonement theology: justice, forgiveness and reconciliation. The article also demonstrates that for human reconciliation to be complete and genuine, all three of these elements are essential. A fourth element, repentance, is also imperative in the process of reconciliation with God. This should be taken as a presupposition to this discussion and is mentioned only occasionally. Repentance is also mostly necessary for reconciliation between people.[92]

Justice without forgiveness cannot produce reconciliation. Forgiveness without reconciliation is possible. But, by

---

[92] Don McLellan, "Justice, Forgiveness, and Reconciliation: Essential Elements in Atonement Theology," *Evangelical Review of Theology* 29 (1): 4–15, 2005, accessed August 5, 2022, https://search-ebscohost-com.wilber forcepayne.idm.oclc.org/login.aspx?direct=true&db=rlh&AN=16206290&site= ehost-live.

definition, it leaves the relationship issues unresolved. And while reconciliation obviously cannot occur without forgiveness, there are important reasons for insisting that when forgiveness is offered, to overlook justice is to endanger the whole concept of forgiveness. These elements cannot be overlooked in the question of reconciliation with God. Reconciliation and atonement are highly congruent to the point of being synonymous. However, the word 'atonement' is more commonly applied to the process of restoring the relationship between humankind and God, rather than between human beings. 'Atonement' is an old English word, derived simply from its elements, 'at- one-ment'. Reconciliation is mostly used of restoring human-to-human relationships, although it is also used with reference to God (1 Corinthians 5:19). Therefore, studying reconciliation may give us important insights into atonement.[93]

At the end of the day, only the biblical theology of substitutionary atonement covers all the bases. Evangelical Christians have always found it difficult to defend; but defend it, they must. The alternatives are wishy-washy forgiveness that produces no time reconciliation, ineffectual justice that trivializes sin, or blunt-instrument justice that perpetuates conflict. Society, and Christianity, can afford none of these.

---

[93] McLellan, "Justice, Forgiveness, and Reconciliation," 5.

BRIDGING THE GAP

Transition is a foundational component of human life and has been a common theme in the church since its inception. Based on the strategic implementation plan, the transition can excite or disturb; it can be healthy or ineffective.[94] This ministry project addresses a systemic concern that derives from a need for more meaningful attention and preparation for the transitional process of pastoral leadership. In addition, this project seeks to explore the adverse emotional and spiritual effects that unhealthy pastoral transition ignites, specifically in conversions concerning sudden departures.

Lastly, this project aims to present a healthy provisional proposal that promotes effective healing and wholeness after experiencing the changing of the pastoral baton. This chapter will provide a pervasive justification for this study by thoroughly investigating empirical and analytical literature

---

[94] R. C. Giambatista, W. G. Rowe, & S. Riaz, "Nothing succeeds like succession: A critical review of leader succession literature since 1994," 2005, *The Leadership Quarterly*, 16(6), 963-991, accessed September 14, 2022, https://doi.org/10.1016/j.leaqua.2005.09.005.

to explain the link between emotional and spiritual wellness and pastoral transition in the Black church. The theoretical basis for this study is Oscar Grusky's succession theories and the mental health and well-being socio-ecological model developed by a team of individuals from various departments at the University of Minnesota.

> *Leaders in the faith-based community must institute tenacious practices that coexist with the church's beliefs and initiate healing and wholeness for congregations across the globe experiencing pastoral transition.*

Pastoral transitions are inevitable; therefore, churches must establish proper guidelines to ensure a smooth process for changing guards and mitigating transitional barriers.[95] Undoubtedly, the world in which we are operating is ever-changing and progressing. Like the forward progression in other areas, the impending transition of a central authority figure is a bureaucratic modification that requires meaningful attention.[96] Leaders in the faith-based community must institute tenacious practices that coexist with the church's beliefs and initiate healing and wholeness for congregations across the globe experiencing pastoral transition. There are many reasons for the transition of a senior leader, including

---

[95] Bryant Wright, *Succession: Preparing Your Ministry for The Next Leader* (Nashville, TN: B&H Books, 2022).

[96] O. Grusky, Administrative succession in formal organizations, *Social Forces*, 39(2), 105, 1960, accessed September 14, 2022, https://doi.org/10.1086/223507.

death, resignation, retirement and by congregational vote.[97] However, regardless of the reason, the departure of a senior leader is unavoidable and has proven to be a difficult adjustment, specifically for lay members.[98]

Oscar Grusky examines the transitions of key leaders, the importance of organizational succession planning, and its impact on the central progression of the institution in his article, *Administrative Succession in Formal Organizations*. Grusky defines succession as the timely election of a suitable candidate to replace a parting chief official. He describes succession as an inevitable managerial disturbance. He argues that every administrative system will undergo succession, but the severity of the change is predicated on the institution's strategic planning strategies and level of endurance. Grusky states, "Succession is disruptive to organizations because it sets the condition for the development of new policies, disturbs the traditional norms of the organization, and promotes changes in the formal and informal relationship among members of the system."[99]

---

[97] J. K. Njoroge, & J. Mwangi, "Assessing factors affecting pastoral leadership transition in churches: A case of evangelical churches in molo sub-county," 2018 *International Journal of Advances Research and Review*, 3(9), 58-72.

[98] Njoroge, & Mwangi, "Assessing factors affecting pastoral leadership," 58-72.

[99] O. Grusky, "Managerial succession and organizational effectiveness," *American Journal of Sociology*, 69(1), 21-31, 1963, accessed September 15, 2022, https://doi.org/10.1086/223507.

Consistent with the principles of Grusky's succession theories, Gina Grandy suggests that saying goodbye to a senior leader, especially one of significant influence, can disarrange the duties of the church, be emotionally alarming, and be spiritually and mentally demanding for the church laity to unravel.[100] In contrast, to the views of Njoroge & Mwangi, Grandy suggests that the transitional process can be equally or even more challenging for the transitioning leader. This is primarily because the African American church's interaction and connection between a senior leader and his flock surpasses a Sunday morning service.

In his book, *Generation to Generation: Family Process in Church and Synagogue (The Guilford Family Therapy Series)*, Edwin Friedman likens the pastor and his congregation to a family. Friedman described the pastor as a spiritual father and an earthly father figure to his sheep. Thus, transitioning leaders and the church laity can experience discomfort, grief, and oversight upon pastoral departure. Incorporating succession planning meetings throughout a pastor's tenure to discuss emergency plans and healthy exit strategies is essential to the church as it can help to alleviate stressors.[101]

---

[100] G. Grandy, "An exploratory study of strategic leadership in churches," 2013, *Leadership and Organization Development Journal*, 34(7), 616-638, accessed September 15, 2022, https://doi. org/10.1108/LODJ-08-2011-0081.

[101] W. Vanderbloemen, & W. Bird, *Next: Pastoral Succession That Works* (Ada, MI: Baker Books, 2013).

In his book *Effective Succession Planning: Ensuring Leadership Continuity and Building Talent from Within*, William Rothwell describes succession planning as the intentional and fundamental attempt by organizational leadership to establish managerial progression in positions of high authority, generate and maintain psychological and scholarly impending resources, and motivate individual and organizational growth.[102]

The absence of proper leadership in positions of superiority leaves a void in the organization and often generates barriers and division within the group. Therefore, something must be put in place that will ultimately aid and assist all involved to ensure forward movement for the church as an organization and for the laypersons who attend. This will allow the church to experience all God has for her

When a senior leader fails to institute a succession plan, chaos and destruction are inevitable during the transitional period.

as God intended without severe damage from a lack of suitable covering. Senior pastors must prepare congregations for the transitional phase to ensure a healthy conversion. Inadequate preparation can decrease the emotional and spiritual wellness of the church laity, have lingering

---

[102] W. J. Rothwell, *Effective Succession Planning: Ensuring Leadership Continuity And Building Talent from Within* 3rd ed. (London, UK: AMACOM, 2005).

adverse effects, and present developmental challenges for both the church members and the incoming pastor.[103]

When a senior leader fails to institute a succession plan, chaos and destruction are inevitable during the transitional period. Implementing practices associated with Grusky's succession theories is critical to the Church as they foresee an agitated society's path and redirect it back to a healthy state.[104] Unfortunately, many predecessors in the Black church do not educate or provide training to their congregations or replacements on proper pastoral succession. Developing traditional systems and formal content to ensure church progression is often disregarded by pastors in the Black church. A common practice in the Christian church is to grasp essential concepts through conversations and experiences rather than creating manuals and developing written action plans.[105]

In his book, *A Change of Pastors: And How It Affects Change in The Congregation*, author Loren B. Mead expresses the importance of transitional support, specifically for individuals who attend religious

---

[103] Wright, *Succession: Preparing Your Ministry.*

[104] D. Botella-Carrubi, & T. Gonzalez-Cruz, T. "Context as a provider of key resources of key resources for succession: A case study of sustainable family firms," *Sustainability*, 11. 1873, accessed September 15 2022, https://doi.org/10.3390/su11071873.

[105] E. C. Lincoln, & L. C. Mamiya, *The Black Church in The African American Experience* (Durham NC: Duke University Press, 1990).

organizations. Through his literary works, Mead provides a practical handbook for religious institutions needing a guide to assist pastors and their congregations in the transitional phase. Mead insists that pastors and congregants need a "how to" directory that provides clarity, direction and steps to employ a healthy transitional course of action.[106] Mead examines the transitional ministry, specifically in the interim period after the pastor's departure and before the successor's appearance. He reveals that the transitional period can be difficult for all parties through his literature. He implies that direction and comfort are necessary for administrative directives, clergy, laity, consultants and pastoral search committees. Mead further explains that the transitional period is a critical time for church laity as essential adjustments take place, and church members are often left feeling disconnected and confused.

Similarly, Molly Dale Smith offers congressional guidance in the book *Transitional Ministry: A Time of Opportunity*.[107] This literary work explains that critical, inevitable, or unforeseen events, such as the transition of a senior leader or even a building fire, can cause friction, devastation and uncertainty within a church. For this reason, faith-based organizations must develop emergency action plans and

---

[106] L. B. Mead, *A Change of Pastors: And How It Affects Change in The Congregation.* (Washington, DC: Rowman & Littlefield, 2014)

[107] M. D. Smith, *Transitional Ministry: A Time of Opportunity* (New York, NY: Church Publishing, 2009).

personnel to aid and assist when critical situations occur. In the absence of a senior leader, transitional ministers can be a significant asset to help steer congregants through the location and selection of a new pastor. In the circumstances involving the loss or resignation of a pastor without a named successor, Smith encourages places of worship to obtain a transitional minister. According to Smith, inviting an experienced transitional minister can assist with creating structural stability throughout the conversion process.[108]

After the transition of a senior pastor, congregations encounter a significant shift in leadership and motivation. The transition of a senior pastor must be handled carefully to prevent further disorder. In her book *Planning in The Small Church: Focusing on Gifts to Fulfill God's Call*, author Laura Stephens-Reed examines the importance of pastoral succession. Reed reports that improper succession burdens the congregation that is no doubt reeling from its current pastor's resignation or predecessor's sudden departure.[109] Senior pastors save their church members from enduring the difficult task of obtaining a transitional minister and initiating a pastoral search when they provide their church with a suitable successor.

---

[108] Smith, *Transitional Ministry.*

[109] L. S. Reed, Planning in *The Small Church: Focusing on Gifts to Fulfill God's Call* (USA: L. S. Reed, 2020).

Moreover, Reed contends that succession is necessary as obtaining an interim pastor can do more harm than good, depending on the church's life cycle. She explains that for churches already on "life support," bringing a short-term minister into the fold only for him to leave soon after can cause even more turmoil to an already weighted and grieving church.[110] According to Reed, throughout the interim period, congregants experience uncertainty and a lack of trust concerning the interim process, the interim pastor, and often each other, causing the ministry to be halted and the attention to be changed from the church's mission and commission to a mode of survival.

Transition Ministries, formerly *Interim Ministries-ABC*, mention that interim pastors help renew and stimulate church laity when no succession plan exists. Program developers at Transition Ministries suggest that interim pastors are beneficial during the transitional period. They can provide church health assessments, initiate preparatory services for congregants upon request, and continue pulpit operations. Conflicting research exists regarding the essentiality of an interim pastor; however, consistent literature surrounds the urgency, necessity, benefits, and health of a church that understands and implements proper succession planning.[111]

---

[110] Reed, *Planning in The Small Church.*

[111] M. D. Smith, (2009). *Transitional Ministry: A Time of Opportunity* (New York, NY: Church Publishing, 2009).

Veteran consultant R. Neil Chafin advises, "How a congregation chooses to use its interim time will shape congregational growth, identity, and health for years to come. We also know that what is done in the interim determines whether the new minister and congregation will form a solid ministry team."[112]

It is important to note that transitional and interim ministers are not synonymous in the context utilized in this project. In this context, transitional ministers refer to those individuals who act as consultants or advisors as they help churches establish a system, continue the vision of the previous pastor, provide pulpit services, and assist the church's search committee in finding a new pastor. On the other hand, an interim pastor is more of a placeholder. The primary job of the interim pastor is to preach to the congregation each week and ensure that church members remain spiritually nourished until the predecessor's replacement is revealed.[113]

Pastoral succession is necessary to discuss as it illustrates the positive effects of proper pastoral transition while simultaneously inferring the consequences of successional negligence. A lack of education and formation concerning the pastoral transition can impact congregants' emotional well-being, causing feelings of brokenness, grief, distrust and

---

[112] Smith, *Transitional Ministry.*
[113] Ibid.

uncertainty.[114] Succession can be viewed as a transitional barrier in faith-based communities that operate as autonomous bodies or independent churches, such as African-independent Pentecostal and Baptist churches. Contrary to historical and conventional churches, the African-independent Pentecostal and Baptist churches do not function on a rotating cycle that requires clergy members to alternate churches after a particular length of time.[115]

Insufficiency regarding successional establishment is so pervasive in the Christian church that congregants and ministry leaders dedicate more time and energy to pastoral search committees than to proper successional practices. Oscar Grusky's succession theories interpret succession as forecasting modifications, creating effective procedures, training, and molding suitable individuals for great responsibility.[116] Although Grusky's succession theories are written from a commercial business approach, the managerial succession practices cf non-profit organizations are comparable in this context.[117]

[114] M. M. Matshobane, M. & M. Masango, "The challenge of pastoral succession in African Independent Pentecostal churches," 2010, *HTS Teologiese Studies/Theological Studies*,76(2), a6265, accessed September 15, 2022, https://doi.org/10.4102/hts.v76i2.6265.

[115] Matshobane & Masango, "The challenge of pastoral succession."

[116] G. Parker, "Succession planning," *Public Garden*, 2018, 33(4), 10.

[117] B. Farah, R. Elias, C. Clercy, & G. Rowe, "Leadership succession in different types of organizations: What business and political successions may learn from each other," 2020, *The Leadership Quarterly*, 3ʲ(1), accessed September 15, 2022, https://doi.org/ 10.1016/j.leaqua.2019.03.004.

Succession planning in faith-based communities is identical to secular organizations as it ensures the timely maintenance and fulfillment of pivotal individuals and positions.[118] In like manner, Armstrong (2003) explains that succession planning is used to justify and occupy vacant chief

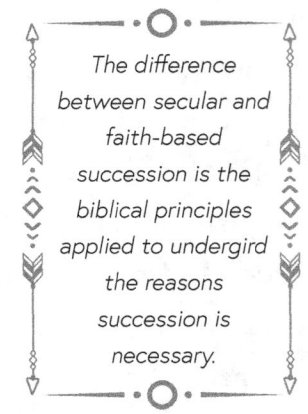

The difference between secular and faith-based succession is the biblical principles applied to undergird the reasons succession is necessary.

positions due to death, voluntary and involuntary withdrawals, or elevation.[119] The difference between secular and faith-based succession is the biblical principles applied to undergird the reasons succession is necessary.

In her article, *Conversion Process in Leadership Succession*, Trudy Heller reasons that the mechanics, repercussions and emotions embedded in the adaptation to new leadership are universal. She illustrates that laws related to spirituality, corporate America, sports, etc., all succumb to the same resolves concerning leadership succession because succession is imminent in every setting.[120] Therefore, the events leading to, and the emotions that stem from succession, are also uniform and inescapable.

---

[118] Parker, "Succession planning," 10.

[119] M. Armstrong, *A Handbook of Human Resource Management Practice*, 9th edition (London, UK: Cambrian Printers, 2003).

[120] T. Heller, "Conversion process in leadership succession: A case study," *The Journal of Applied Behavioral Science*, 25(1), 65-77, 1989, accessed September 15, 2022. https://doi.org/10.1177/00 21886389251005.

The process model of succession provides a comprehensive insight into the formalities people endure amid leadership transformation [121] Institutional formalities provide structure and act as a guide for church congregants. Developmental insufficiencies regarding shifts in the pastoral position cause disruptions to the daily flow and functionality of the church. [22] In contrast, Grusky's succession theories demonstrate that even when the proper groundwork has been applied to ensure managerial succession, disruption will likely occur, often leading to significant functional and dysfunctional outcomes.[123] The literature reports that the need for succession in the faith-based community is paramount as the average length of tenure steadily declines.[124]

The increased number of pastoral transitions in the Black church does not indicate the number of pastoral succession plans. In their book, *Next: Pastoral Succession That Works*, Vanderbloemen and Bird reveal that eighty-four percent of religious institutions do not have proper succession practices for their pastor. Vanderbloemen and Bird suggest that senior leaders are not prepared for succession due to the absence

---

[121] C. A. Tucker, "Succession planning for academic nursing," *Journal of Professional Nursing*, 36(5), 334-342, 2020.

[122] M Ritchie, Succession planning for successful leadership: Why we need to talk about succession planning! "Management in Education," 34(1), 2020.

[123] Giambatista, Rowe, & Riaz, Nothing succeeds like succession," 963-991.

[124] Farah, Elias, Clercy, & Rowe, "Leadership succession."

of monetary forecasting, a sense of uneasiness concerning the release of the church, and anxiety regarding life after pastoral ministry.[125] This mindset causes pastors to dismiss successional agendas and recede from initiating proper transitional planning. When clergy leaders do not adequately plan for succession, their flock is abandoned and exposed, making them vulnerable to satanic attacks. Additionally, successional negligence displays poor stewardship and a lack of spiritual maturity for clergy leaders.

Strong pastoral transitions are vital in the life of the church. A poor transition can have lasting repercussions, such as loss of church members, damage to the integrity and reputation of the church, and cultivate significant challenges for the new administration.[126] Succession theories were designed to forecast the process of conversion within an ecological society over time. Consistent with research by Oscar Grusky, researchers Botella-Carrubi, and Gonzalez-Cruz, reveals that succession theories offer a theoretical ideology to advise and communicate restorative protocols.[127]

Grusky's succession theories are vital to undergirding this project and relevant to ongoing research as it offers

---

[125] Vanderbloemen, & Bird, *Next: Pastoral Succession That Work.*

[126] P. Bunton, "Reflexivity in practical theology: reflections from studies of founders' succession in Christian organizations," *Practical Theology,* 12(1), 2019, accessed September 15, 2022, https://doi.org/10.1080/1756073X.2019.1575039.

[127] Botella-Carrubi, & Gonzalez-Cruz, (2019). Context as a provider, 11.

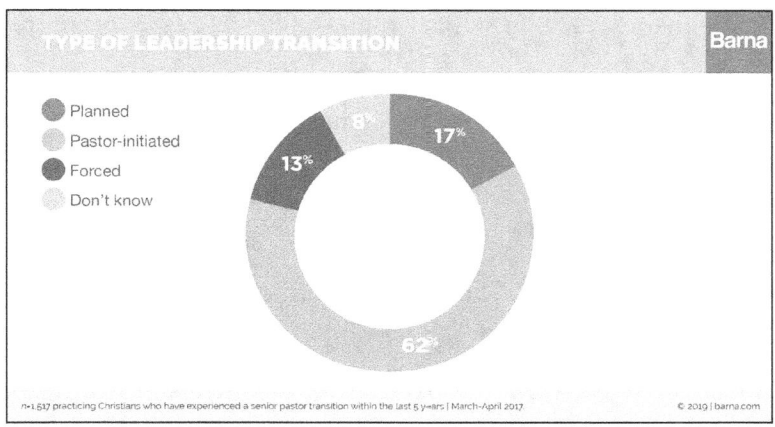

Figure 1 Type of Leadership Transition

extensive insight into the positive effects of proper transitions while simultaneously inferring the adverse effects of a lack thereof. It is the goal of this ministry project to consider Grusky's succession theories to help senior leaders, and their congregations understand the value of proper succession planning, and the emotional and organizational turmoil that stems from inadequate transitional plans and successional negligence. The hope is that senior leaders and their ministry teams will begin to address preparatory procedures consistently and intentionally for the transitional process of senior pastors. Suitable transitional procedures must generate effective coping mechanisms and contribute to the holistic growth of the church. An effective succession plan begins at the start of a pastor's tenure and ends after the new pastor has been installed.[128] At this time, the new pastor and his administrative team should create his succession plan to ensure continued structural balance and movement.

Barna analysts separated pastoral successions into three distinct categories founded upon the events impacting the administrative shift. "The first is planned transitions, which are planned of the change (17%); the second is pastor-initiated transitions, set into motion by a decision from the outgoing pastor (62%); and the third is forced transitions, commenced by unexpected circumstances such as illness, death, or crisis (13%)" (www.barna.com)."

Senior pastors and their administrative staff must understand that the post-emotional and spiritual well-being of the congregation significantly impacts the victory surrounding the changing of the pastoral guard.

Pastor-initiated transitions are the most prominent. Moreover, while illness, death and crisis may be the lowest percentage regarding these pastoral transitions, they make up some of the most challenging adjustments that faith-based institutions have endured. Where does that leave the congregation? How long do they wait before getting another pastor? Do they desire another pastor? What type of healing needs to occur during the transition, and where will that leave the people and the

---

[128] Ritchie, "Succession planning for successful leadership."

leadership? These are just a few questions we are to navigate to ensure a settling solution for the people of God and their continued progress toward destiny.

Pastors and critical church leaders are the driving force behind creating a strategic successional plan. Equipping an institution for managerial transition requires coaching, discipline, strong communication, and a written instructional manual reviewed annually.[129] Senior pastors and their administrative staff must understand that the post-emotional and spiritual well-being of the congregation significantly impacts the victory surrounding the changing of the pastoral guard. Therefore, this ministry project's goal remains to educate senior leaders on the significance of proper succession planning and reveal that the faith-based community will lose its spiritual and emotional vitality if the facilitation and embedding of holistic healing and wholeness are not implemented throughout the pastoral transition process.

An in-depth description of the pastoral role in the Black church is necessary to understand the connection between pastoral transition and emotional and spiritual wellness. Pastors have a significant role in their congregants' and local communities' lives. Black clergy leaders are often spiritual advisors, friends, counselors, father figures and mentors to

---

[129] M. Sherrer and D. Rezania, "A scoping review on the use and effectiveness of leadership coaching in succession planning," *International Journal of Theory, Research, and Practice*, 13(2), 2020.

many individuals in their flock. Senior leaders with lengthy tenures have witnessed their young people grow up and start their own families.[130] The reality is that by the time a clergy leader in the Black church transitions from his role as pastor, he has married and buried many of his congregants and their loved ones, established relationships with those in the local community, including neighbors and business owners, participated as a character witness in legal cases, conducted hospital visits, and more. Additionally, many African American senior leaders serve as political activists for the Black community. It is the commission and pursuit of many churches to serve beyond the spiritual realm and spread to other domains, including social, economic and political.[131]

In his book, *The Black Church: This Is Our Story, This Is Our Song*, Henry Louis Gates, Jr. resolved that, for centuries, senior leaders in the Black church, and the entire African American faith-based community, are recognized as the cornerstone of Black neighborhoods. Gates explains that Black pastors are foundational components in the lives of their flock, and he argues that Black pastors have always been more than just the average minister. Gates indicates that Black pastors and ministers have had a pivotal role in the community, with many doubling as pastors and civil

---

[130] B. E. Harmon, S. Strayhorn, B. L. Webb, & J. R. Hébert, "Leading God's people: Perceptions of influence among African American pastors," *Journal of Religion and Health*, 57(4), 1509–1523, 2018, https://doi.org/10.1007/s10943-018- 0563-9.

[131] Harmon, Strayhorn, Webb, & JHébert, "Leading God's people."

rights activists for years.[132] Similarly, in his book, *Black Redemption: Churchmen Speak for the Garvey Movement*, Randall Burkett states that Black pastors play a significant role in the lives of those they guard over, including those in the communities they serve. Burkett argues that a Black pastor is the most influential person in the community as he oversees the community's most powerful institution.[133]

According to Masenya, new and emerging generations expect African American pastors to prioritize mental health awareness and acknowledge major health factors impacting the Black community due to the ongoing socioeconomic inequities, poverty and racial injustice.[134] Conversely, Gates

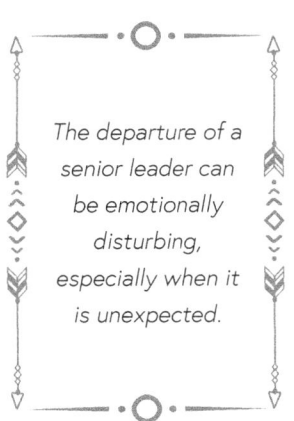

The departure of a senior leader can be emotionally disturbing, especially when it is unexpected.

argues that engaging Black pastors in matters that plague the Black community is not new. He contends that African American pastors have been the voice of the Black community for decades, spanning back to the times of Reverend Dr. Martin Luther King, Jr. and other senior leaders who

---

[132] H. L. Gates, Jr., *The Black Church: This Is Our Story, This Is Our Song* (New York, NY: Penguin Press, 2021).

[133] R. K. Burkett, *Black Redemption: Churchmen Speak For The Garvey Movement*, 1st ed. (Philedelphia, PA: Temple University Press, 1978).

[134] M. J. Masenya, "Caught between the sacred and the secular: The pentecostal pastor as a leader in a world in constant flux," 49(1), 115-132, 2021, accessed April 2, 2023, https://doi. org/10.7832/49-0-425churches.

came before, such as Dr. Benjamin Elijah Mays, Reverend C. L. Franklin, and George Alexander McGuire.[135]

The departure of a senior leader can be emotionally disturbing, especially when it is unexpected. Leading emotionally and spiritually bruised congregants requires intentional care from incoming pastors to combat the transitional barriers associated with the departure of the previous administration. Jeannie Duck, the author of *Change Monster*, reveals that navigating a pastoral transition is a formidable and vulnerable time for the laity and the new pastor.

In the article, *Organizational Change and Self-Concept Thoughts*, researchers Eilam & Shamir revealed that institutional adjustments could be deferred, postponed and often unsuccessful due to employees' psychological struggles to acknowledge, receive, welcome and adapt to new modifications. According to Eilam & Shamir, the incoming administration must identify the critical issues impacting the forward movement of the laity and the church at large.[136]

New pastors must also seek to integrate past leadership methods with new ones and not dismiss the last

---

[135] Masenya, "Caught between the sacred and the secular."

[136] G. Eilam, B. & Shamir, "Organizational change and self-concept threats. *The Journal of Applied Behavioral Science*, 41(4), 399-421, 2005, accessed September 15, 2022, https://doi.org/10. 1177/002 1886305280865.

administration.[137] Doing so helps congregants cope better with the absence of the old administration while welcoming a new leader with differing leadership approaches.[138] On the contrary, researchers Mdletye, Coerzee & Ukpere believe that new pastors should lead with their vision to keep from getting lost in the vision of their predecessor or experiencing ongoing demand from the laity to lead the same way as the previous administration.

The Socio-Ecological Model of Mental Health and Well-being identifies the components that intersect and influence various areas of life. These components have a diverse effect on people as the level of influence is based on the degree of

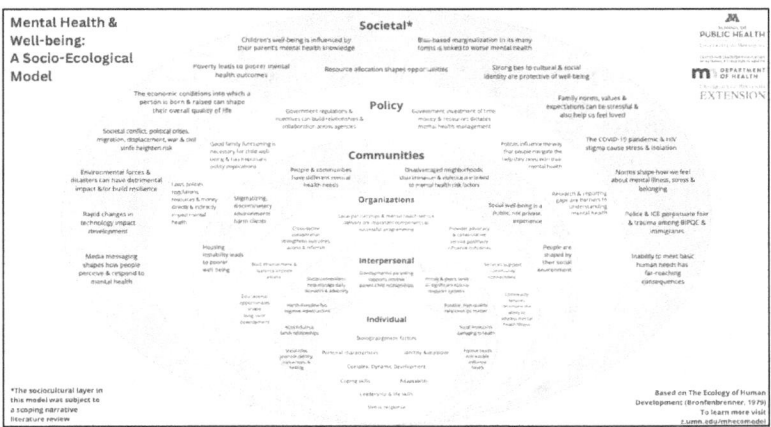

Figure 2 Mental Health and Well-Being:
A Socio-Ecological Model

---

[137] A. Son, "Anxiety as a main cause of church conflicts based on Bowen family systems theory," *Journal of Pastoral Care & Counseling,* 73(1), 9–18, 2019, https://doi.org/10.1177/154230 5018822959.

[138] Son, "Anxiety as a main cause of church conflicts."

the interchange.[139] Undergirded by Urie Bronfenbrenner's ecology of human development, the social-ecological model of mental health and well-being suggests that a person's societal circumstances, individuality, organizational, family and communal origins shape one's mental health and well-being.[140] The factors introduced in socio-ecological theories are significant to the growth and justification behind human dependency and persistence, specifically in the event of substantial and communal disturbance.[141] The transition of a clergyman is likened to a form of grief due to the death of the relationship.

In his book, *How Your Church Family Works: Understanding Congregations As Emotional Systems*, Peter Steinke suggests that people are communal beings, and communities, including faith-based ministries, create a structure that connects and motivates one another significantly.[142] Steinke implies that when communities of

---

[139] Cari Michaels, Linda Blake, Anna Lynn, Teale Greylord, and Sara Benning, "Mental Health and Well-Being Ecological Model," *Center for Leadership Education in Maternal & Child Public Health*, University of Minnesota–Twin Cities, April 18, 2022, accessed September 15, 2022, https://mch.umn.edu/resources/mhecomodel/.

[140] Michaels, Blake, Lynn, Greylord, and Benning, "Mental Health and Well-Being Ecological Model."

[141] S. Y. Neely-Fairbanks, L. Rojas-Guyler, L. Nabors, & L. Banjo, "Mental illness knowledge, stigma, help-seeking behaviors, spirituality and the African American church," *American Journal of Health Studies*, 33(4), 162-174, 2018, access September 15, 2022, https://doi.org/10.47779/ajhs .2018.69.

[142] P. L. Steinke, *How Your Church Family Works: Understanding Congregations As Emotional Systems* (Herndon, VA: Alban Institute, 2006), 17.

great significance encounter unexpected modifications, emotional and psychological reactions are sure to follow.

Additionally, he explains that humans are repetitious creatures by nature, making it hard for people to adjust to change. Thus, Steinke submits that faith-based leaders must fully comprehend the systematic structure of the mind, including the cognitive and spiritual components, before indelible adjustments can occur.[143]

When change occurs, incredibly immediate and unforeseen, culture is one of the first things that shifts.

When asked about the future of the church, Pastor Rick Warren revealed, "I believe the key issue for churches in the twenty-first century will be church health, not church growth." Leading change in the church is not about spirituality alone, but integrating spirituality, faith, and emotional, mental and physical processes into one's leadership style to ensure a holistic ministry.

A pastoral transition is affected by multiple components, requiring an examination of various areas of congregational wellness. The sectors of the church that commonly experience the most trauma due to religious change include culture, economics, social climate, and emotional state and

---

[143] Steinke, *How Your Church Family Works*, 17.

well-being. A professor of sociology of religion, Nancy Ammerman, states, "It is not unusual for the people who gather into a congregation to share a common social and cultural heritage." Thus, suggesting that multiple age groups and family generations make up the church's infrastructure. Pastoral transition causes upheaval and separation of these families due to differing emotional stances. Some family members leave the family church and join other households of faith, while others leave the faith-based community altogether. When change occurs, incredibly immediate and unforeseen, culture is one of the first things that shifts. Things are no longer the same, creating an uptick in the normalcy of the congregation.

Changes of this magnitude lead to economic distress and often create significant concerns regarding the lack of financial support, ultimately stifling the church's ability to uphold financial obligations. The pressure of keeping finances without a leader is not always the most incredible experience, especially when it is an unplanned pastoral transition. Faith is sometimes stunted. Growth is not the order of the day. Consistency in different areas of the church is lacking, and there are times when a once vibrant and working church must undergo losses in many places. Finances are one of the greatest losses often. Economic turmoil and distress, in addition to cultural shifts and changes, can lead to declining membership, a dip in efforts for responsible ministry, and sometimes the church doors being closed altogether. Money is not everything to a church or congregation; but it means something when it is time to do work, and there are no resources. This can ultimately be very emotional for anyone, especially those who decide to stay at the church during the pastoral transition.

Finally, one would need to consider the laity's emotions in the different sectors affected by the pastoral transition. Spanning beyond the congregation, the shifts in ministry do not have to end in death for one's emotions to erupt. Upon the transition of a senior leader, any length carries the weight of emotional repercussions. After the pastoral transition, it is common for church members to stop attending worship at their local assembly and eventually, unfortunately, leave the faith-based community altogether. Some members may become inactive, while others will do the bare minimum to get by. This critical component can have a residual impact without a proper solution.

A specific plan must assist the church in governing itself until another leader is selected and throughout the introductory pastoral phase. Churches that have been in operation for long periods of time, especially Black Baptists, have had phenomenal leaders who left their churches in disarray due to the lack of planning regarding pastoral succession. No faith-based assembly should ever be left without a leader. When that happens, a negative aspect halts and stunts what is to come for that church. When a new leader comes into play by immediate selection or a majority voting process, they come in with a thought process and perspective that things are one way when they are something altogether different. More often than not, the new pastor comes in at a significant disadvantage, and there is little to no regard for the success of their now-piloted efforts to move the church forward.

Wesse and Cartree explain that a pragmatic strategy must be incorporated into a transition plan. They further explain that protective measures must be put into place to shield the congregation from emotional, physical and spiritual trauma amid a pastoral transition, particularly in sudden transitions such as the death of a senior leader. Experts agree that there is no "one size fits all" for a succession plan. However, foundational principles can be implemented to make the transition process manageable.[144]

New ideas are present. New initiatives are in motion. New people are in office, and new mindsets are at the helm. Further movement is taking place. A new focus is at the table. New planning is being executed, and other sacrifices are being made for the overall achievement of the church. "With the number of conflicts that can arise from pastoral

---

[144] Matshobane & Masango, "The challenge of pastoral succession."

transition, it should be no surprise that congregations go through a myriad of reactions upon learning that the pastor is resigning or transitioning in another way." Although it is no surprise, everything experienced must be done with the congregation in mind.

This often transpires due to the response reflecting the attitude and disposition of shocked people who are now aware of the difference in relationship and experience of what has occurred. Dealing with an unplanned transition translates into a time of liability, frailty, dereliction and congregational discord. The abruptness of demise, dysfunction or disorder of the pastor's body, hasty exit, or expulsion will not allow the congregation the time of grieving necessary to reassess their cultural and traditional customs. It won't allow the congregation to reinvent who they are and what they bring to the community in which they reside. It won't allow the congregation to take another look at their vision to reimagine their innovation for the days, weeks, months and years to come.

In times of transition, the social change of a church manifests properly when community members receive the support necessary to deal with their spiritual and emotional needs.

There will need to be conversations on what the church will look for in a new leader. The body has to express what they will accept and turn away, and what type of authority they will allow them to have. The issues discussed serve as the launching pad for structured pastoral transition, what it looks like, and why it is essential to do it right. When pastoral change occurs, it needs to be done from a healthy standpoint. It needs to be productive for congregational growth, while honoring where they are, along with help and guidance to get them where they need to be.

This ministry project seeks to provide a guide for churches that are experiencing pastoral transition. I suggest that proper transitional planning preserves the necessary leadership while healthily welcoming a new administration to ensure the church meets current and future organizational needs throughout the transitional period. In times of transition, the social change of a church manifests properly when community members receive the support necessary to deal with their spiritual and emotional needs. When preparation ensues for moments of pastoral transition, and proper practices are implemented to combat the social-emotional factors attached, faith-based communities can anticipate a sustainable and healthy future with the new administration. I believe that providing coping strategies is crucial for the new pastor and the church. Engaging in activities such as "group therapy" can help all parties navigate the good and bad that stem from pastoral transition.

Ministry leaders who continue through a pastoral transition should ask themselves, "How can we honor the outgoing pastor while simultaneously setting the incoming pastor up to win?" A new pastor might ask, "How do I lead a church with a vision I did not create and a ministry staff I did not put in place?" A current pastor may also ask, "Am I equipped to lead my church through a healthy transition?"

It is the goal of this ministry project to consider Grusky's succession theories and the Socio-Ecological Model of Mental Health and Well-being to help senior leaders and their congregations understand the value of proper succession planning and provide a comprehensive connection between pastoral transition and socio-emotional trauma. This ministry adds to the existing body of literature as it suggests an art to proper pastoral transition and offers a pervasive blueprint to new pastors that can be used to facilitate the institution of effective healing amid pastoral transition.

How does implementing Grusky's succession theories help equip senior leaders with the knowledge and tools necessary to create proper transition protocols and implement proper succession planning after years of successional negligence? Can the Socio-Ecological Model of Mental Health and Well-being be the catalyst necessary to ensure a healthy and holistic pastoral transition? How do new pastors facilitate effective healing for congregations after the pastoral transition? What strategies can be implemented to promote effective healing and wholeness in the church? These are the guiding questions for this ministry project and for those experiencing this top-heavy situation and circumstance.

A New Approach to Pastoral Succession

In time, the past administration at Faith Church announced to the congregation that they were ready to explore other options in life. During the last few years, the church was dwindling, not necessarily changing with the times. There were some stark differences in the way the church was being run in comparison to when this administration first started. While in the transition stage, and the separation of pastor and people coming up soon, there were some promises made to that particular leader that could not really be fulfilled because of the decline in membership. With the decline in membership came a decline in revenue. The board said, "If we can give a good send-off, our ability not to give what was purposed and desired and all that comes with it could be forgiven." It is said that the leader consented.

Whatever was agreed upon shifted. Sometime after separation, the leader engaged in legal action with Faith Church. This was probably one of the most trying times that Faith Church had to endure. At this point, the church was pastor-less with a lingering debt hanging over their heads. However, a few years later, while still having to endure what was going on, a new leader was placed in position.

Although God has given Faith Church good success over the years, the separation of the previous administration placed the congregation in a very vulnerable position as the deacon board of the church was thrusted into leadership over the church for a number of years until a new leader was selected. The process of selecting a new pastor was an old standard in the Black Baptist church, one that has certainly benefited the church in the past but stood in need of a radical upgrade.

It did not take long to assess the process, which resulted in a new leader being called to pastor Faith Church. It was decided that the process used to select the new leader should not occur to Faith Church, or any other pastors and churches. Consequently, research was conducted by way of theoretical foundations to determine the best method and best practices available for pastoral transition or succession. What I discovered was unprecedented in the traditional Black Baptist church. I implemented a pastoral succession plan for the church, giving the entire congregation the opportunity to transition with the person selected to become their next pastor while the current pastor was still in place and still very much engaged in the day-to-day operations and decision-making of the church.

While pastoral successions are not new in the Black Baptist church, the process Faith Church created and implemented for their congregation is. Traditionally, after a long-standing pastoral tenure, if that pastor had a son or relative in pastoral ministry, they would be chosen with minimal opposition to succeed the reigning pastor. While this is a way to bring about succession, it has significant flaws that have not served those churches who have used this model well, especially when considering the percentage of those churches where the plan worked well.

The heuristic hypothesis was if a biblical model of healing that leads to pastoral succession is implemented, it would assist in congregational trust, belief, management, healing and wholeness. The project tested its heuristic hypothesis using a mixed method model consisting of pre/posttest, sermon and a Bible study.

The use of a pre- and post-test determined the level of knowledge gained throughout the learning process. By assessing current knowledge prior to exposure, and knowledge gained after learning, these tests provided information on project content, understanding, value and teaching methods. This information was useful when considering if this level of engagement should be taken in the future or modified as a part of action research.

Sermons are the bedrock of the church and the Gospel. Sermons are the most effective way to share the Word of God. Using a sermon to illuminate the biblical text and shed light on the context's ability to adhere to God's Word is the most effective way to modify current behavior, culture and systems toward a more preferred method.

The Bible study allowed the project participants to learn, interpret and be transformed by applying God's Word to successful succession models. As participants gain confidence and trust in God's method of resolving succession issues, they will be able to encourage other members to get involved and become transformed, as well.

Each of the selected methods will be analyzed based on the proposed heuristic hypothesis individually, then collectively to determine any patterns of consistency or inconsistency. The goal is for consistency across all four methods of testing.

PRE- AND POST-TEST QUESTIONNAIRE

The pre-test questionnaire examined the existing level of knowledge participants have about succession, hurt, pain and trauma, and their impact on the overall health of the congregation.

At the end of the project, when all testing and learning has been completed, a post-test was administered using the same questions as the pre-test. The results of the pretest were compared to the results from the post-test to determine the overall level of learning of the participants. Closer examinations occurred with questions that had the greatest deviation to assess the validity of probing deeper into those areas for greater clarification and explanation.

I expected that the results from the pre- and post-test questionnaires would indicate an increase in knowledge toward the importance and value of succession plans toward making pastoral changes. I also expected that the results would show a desire on the part of the participants to move toward transforming pain and hurt into the wholeness of the congregation.

THE SERMON

The sermon would be taken from the Old Testament book of Joshua. The sermon text was taken from the biblical foundation and what happens when leadership change is done according to God's plan.

Joshua 1:1-18

The Lord commissioned Joshua as Moses' successor to lead Israel into the promised land. God instructed Joshua to be obedient to the law of Moses and to be courageous so that he might succeed. Joshua commanded the officers of the camp to prepare the people for crossing the Jordan. He reminded the Transjordan tribes of Reuben, Gad and the half-tribe of Manasseh that they had committed themselves under Moses to cross and help their brothers. The people agreed and echoed the exhortation of God to Joshua, "Only be strong and courageous!"

The outline of the text is as follows:

1. God encourages his leader.

2. The leader encourages the officers.

3. The officers encourage the leader.

Questions from Joshua 1:1-18

On a scale of 1-5, rate the following statements as they apply to your context of ministry. These questions pertain to your understanding of the biblical text in relationship to biblical succession.

1=highly disagree   2=disagree   3=neutral   4=agree   5=highly agree

Questions	Rating (% answered)
I did not fully understand the meaning of the sermon before it was preached.	1 2 3 4 5
The sermon changed my understanding of the text.	1 2 3 4 5
I was convicted by the sermon that was preached.	1 2 3 4 5
The sermon empowered me to action.	1 2 3 4 5
I am more aware of the importance of succession.	1 2 3 4 5
More members of the church need to hear this sermon.	1 2 3 4 5

BIBLE STUDY

The Bible study was based on what occurs in the life of the people of God when biblical succession is followed according to God's plan for God's people. The purpose of the sermons and Bible studies using the same text was to allow the participants to drill down into the text for greater clarity and understanding. The Bible study, like the sermon, focused on uncovering the hermeneutical meaning for practical application in the project context.

Questions from Joshua 1:1-18

On a scale of 1-5, rate the following statements as they apply to your context of ministry. These questions pertain to your understanding of the biblical text in relationship to the effects of multi-layered encouragement.

1=highly disagree   2=disagree   3=neutral   4=agree   5=highly agree

Questions	Rating (% answered)
I did not fully understand the meaning of the Bible study before it was taught.	1 2 3 4 5
The Bible study changed my understanding of the text.	1 2 3 4 5
I was convicted by the Bible study that was taught.	1 2 3 4 5
The Bible study empowered me to action.	1 2 3 4 5
I am more aware of the importance of succession.	1 2 3 4 5
More members of the church need to be taught this lesson.	1 2 3 4 5

EXPECTED RESULTS

A tremendous amount of time and effort went into the design and development of this project. First and foremost, the contextual analysis that was developed in the first semester of this program was critical in how the project was designed. Without conducting the appropriate level of research on existing methods of succession, churches will continue to suffer from making ill-advised pastoral selections.

The project has been developed to make sure that everyone who wishes to participate could. It also took into consideration the educational level, reading comprehension, and ability to express ideas and important thoughts. The members of Faith Church who volunteered to participate have been true angels. With the wealth of work that needed to be done in various areas and at various times, this project would not have been possible without their input.

IN THE FIELD
LIFE APPLICATION

F aith Church is a congregation that has experienced the joys of a long, substantial pastoral relationship with its former leader who announced his time of departure from service to their congregation. After, the leader legally opposed the congregation for things beyond their control, putting the congregation in financial distress. This action also made it difficult for Faith Church to secure a new leader; therefore, the deacons assumed leadership for a little over a few years. This action further eroded the confidence of existing members, reducing worship attendance and weekly financial offerings.

Ultimately, the church called their next pastor. The new leadership and administration inherited the responsibility of healing a painfully wounded and fractured congregation. Knowing the horrors of the traditional call system of the Black Baptist church firsthand, I sought to change the methodology of pastoral changes, regardless of the reason for the needed change. After prayer and soul-searching, I decided to abandon the traditional methodology of calling the next pastor and implement a pastoral succession plan designed to select the most effective pastoral replacement with minimal negative effect on the congregation.

Methodology

T he methodology was based on a mixed method and data triangulation approach using a pre- and post-test questionnaire, sermon and Bible study to ascertain relevant data to test the heuristic hypothesis.

What follows is a summary of the field work performed at Faith Church. The findings will be presented based on the three methods of testing, followed by an overall assessment of the findings.

Pre- & Post-test

The pre- and post-test consisted of two sets of five questions. The first set was for the pre-test, and the second set was for the post-test. The pre-test questionnaire was administered at the conclusion of the introduction to the ministry project. There was a total of ten participants: five male and five females. Both male and female participants varied in length of time they have been active members of Faith Church, ranging from five to over fifty years. The purpose of the pre-test was to gain insight on the level of knowledge the participants had regarding selecting a new pastor and its impact on the life of the church. Below are the results of the pre-test.

On a scale of 1-5, rate the following statements as they apply to your context of ministry. These questions pertain to your understanding of the biblical text in relationship to the command of God to be obedient.

1=highly disagree   2=disagree   3=neutral   4=agree   5=highly agree

Questions	Rating (% answered)				
I understand the process for changing pastors at Faith Church.	40	50	10	0	0
	64	24	12	0	0
The recommended pastoral change process will make a positive impact on the congregation.	49	26	20	5	0
	49	24	18	9	0
The pastoral change process needs to be updated and improved to better serve the congregation and community.	49	39	12	0	0
	59	12	24	5	0
The prior pastoral change process created hurt among the membership.	41	19	15	11	14
	29	12	12	29	18
The right pastoral succession plan will provide maximum continuity for the congregation going forward.	3	14	4	17	62
	6	6	6	24	59

Analysis of Pre- & Post-Test

An initial review of the results of the pre-test indicated that most of the participants were aware of the process of changing pastors at Faith Church. When asked if the participants understood the process, 40% of the audience highly agreed and 50% agreed. This meant that over 90% of the participants were familiar with the way pastors are called at Faith Church. On the post-test, the "highly agree" category increased by 24% to 64%. Overall, these percentages indicated a mature level of the administrative structure of Faith Church.

When asked if the recommended pastoral change process would make a positive impact on the congregation, the pre- and post-test participants responded that 49% highly agreed; 24% agreed on the pre-test and 26% agreed on the post-test. This would indicate that nearly two-thirds of the participants believed that the recommended pastoral change process would have a positive impact on the church. Neutral responses by participants were 20% and 18%, respectively, on the pre- and the post-test. When asked if the pastoral change process needed to be updated to better serve the church and community, the "highly agree" category went from 49% to 59%, and the "agree" category went from 30% to 12%. The difference between the pre- and post-test appeared in the neutral category. Neutral responses went from 12% to 24%.

Sermon

The sermon from the book of Joshua demonstrated how God systematically and pragmatically shifted the leadership of God's people from Moses to Joshua. On a scale of 1-5, rate the following statements as they apply to your context of ministry. These questions pertain to your understanding of the biblical text in relationship to the command of God to be strong and courageous.

1=highly disagree   2=disagree   3=neutral   4=agree   5=highly agree

Questions (**Joshua 1:1-18**)	**Rating** (% answered)				
I did not fully understand the meaning of the sermon before it was preached.	50	30	10	10	
The sermon changed my understanding of the text.	90	10			
I was convicted by the sermon that was preached.				20	80
The sermon empowered me to action.			10	60	30
I am more aware of the importance of succession.	90	10			
More members of the church need to hear this sermon.	30	30	20	20	

The results of the first sermon indicated that 80% of the participants either highly agreed or agreed that they did not fully understand the meaning of the sermon before it was preached. This would indicate that, while this text was a very familiar text, the implications of the text were either vague, had multiple meanings, or the participants could not relate to the text in its original context.

After the sermon was preached, 90% of the participants highly agreed that their understanding of the text changed and 10% of the participants agreed that their understanding of the text changed. This would indicate that, while most of the participants did not understand the meaning of the text prior to the sermon being preached, the content of the sermon provided clarity about the text's meaning. In cases like this, hermeneutics and vivid illustrations provide a contextual framework for participants to understand the meaning of the text being preached. This is often the case with congregations where members are unfamiliar with significant biblical passages.

Even though 90% of the participants understood the meaning of the text after it was preached, 80% indicated that the sermon did not convict them. Additionally, 60% did not agree that the sermon empowered them to action. Significant to the sermon was that 90% of the participants indicated that they were more aware of succession after the sermon was preached.

Bible Study

A Bible study was taught as a part of this ministry project. Each study was taught after the sermon was preached to give the participants an opportunity to drill down on the subject matter for greater clarity.

On a scale of 1-5, rate the following statements as they apply to your context of ministry.

1=highly disagree   2=disagree   3=neutral   4=agree   5=highly agree

Questions (Joshua 1:1-18)	Rating (% answered)				
I did not fully understand the meaning of the text before it was taught.				70	30
The lesson changed my understanding of the text.			100		
I was convicted by the lesson that was preached.			50	50	
The lesson empowered me to action.				70	30
I am more aware of the importance of succession.			100		
More members of the church need to be taught this lesson.			100		

On a scale of 1-5, rate the following statements as they apply to your context of ministry. These questions pertain to your understanding of the biblical text in relationship to the command of God to be strong and courageous.

1=highly disagree   2=disagree   3=neutral   4=agree   5=highly agree

Questions (**Joshua 1:1-18**)	Rating (% answered)
I did not fully understand the meaning of the lesson before it was taught.	20 80
The lesson changed my understanding of the text.	80 20
I was convicted by the lesson that was taught.	90 10
The lesson empowered me to action.	100
I am more aware of the importance of succession.	100
More members of the church need to be taught this lesson.	100

The results of the Bible study indicated growth in the participants' understanding of the importance of succession or itineracy. The responses to the questions significantly improved from those of the sermon series because the participants were familiar with the biblical text that was taught. Preaching a sermon followed by Bible study on the same text has proven to be an effective way to increase biblical literacy, ministry possibility, and a path forward toward resolving congregational problems. Since the results of the Bible study showed improvement from the sermon, there was no reason to provide a detailed analysis of the results.

Success & Significance

Once the pre- and post-tests, sermon and Bible study were completed, the final step in the data analysis was to perform a data triangulation on the various testing instruments. The goal of the data triangulation was to compare the various testing instruments to see if there were any significant deviations in the overall testing data from one instrument to another.

The sermon and Bible study were very similar in how they were answered. Most of the respondents had difficulty understanding the sermon text prior to the sermon being preached, and the sermon did not empower them to take any action toward pastoral succession planning. However, once the sermon was preached, and the Bible study was taught, there were notable changes in the participants who highly agreed that they understood the text prior to the study and that the subject matter empowered them to action.

In all cases, the participants agreed that more people in the congregation should be exposed to the projects preaching and teaching segments. Additionally, there was minimal familiarization of the biblical text in the beginning. But, by the end of each segment, participants agreed that they had gained an appreciation and awareness of the importance of succession.

The tests indicated measurable increases in knowledge from the pre- to the post-test. This is an indication that the sermon and Bible study were well received, and the data presented made an impression on the participants. The areas that participants were least aware of showed the greatest amount of improvement; again, a testimony to the level of excellence that went into each presentation.

Overall, the project was a tremendous success in illuminating for the congregation the importance of succession planning as the preferred method of choosing new pastors for Faith Church and the prayer is that it stands as a foundational structure that will aid and assist any other ministry if implemented correctly and with fidelity.

CONCLUSION

M y ministry project was a success due to the support and assistance from a vast number of people. Reflecting on my spiritual journey has allowed me to see the burdens that God has lifted from my life, enabling me to go and be a blessing to others. My spiritual journey has also enabled me to see the difference between my life's work and my ministry. My life's work is based on burdens lifted, and my ministry is based on the job description of the pastor. Knowing these differences helps me empower my ministry leaders to lead based on the spiritual journey and serve the church based on their giftings.

Enlightenment from doing foundational research gave me confidence in creating a model of pastoral succession that was biblically, historically, theologically and theoretically consistent. The foundations affirmed the necessity, assurance and benefits of pastoral succession, which allowed the participants and congregation to make the decision to adopt my pastoral succession plan for Faith Church without hesitation.

The participants for my field work, the context, and professional associates worked well together. Learning took place at every level of the project implementation. Understanding the uncertainty of when a pastoral change is necessary empowered the participants to affirm an ongoing process of pastoral succession as Faith Church is led and guided, as God gives direction. At the end of the process emerged a replicable model of ministry that will be institutionalized in the life of Faith Church and your church, as well.

Replicable Pastoral Succession Model of Ministry

The culmination of this promising work is to develop a replicable model of ministry. The replicable model of ministry was the key component of my research, in that it allows me to add to the existing body of knowledge so that the kingdom of God can be advanced at Faith Church and throughout the country.

There is no such thing as a one-size-fits-all transition plan.

The model consists of the following steps:

1. **Perspective: Get the real picture.**

    There is no such thing as a one-size-fits-all transition plan. Don't think you can follow what some other pastor or other church did that seemed to work for them. It will not work for you. Every church, outgoing pastor and incoming pastor, staff, board and congregation are unique. Successful leadership transition is more of an art than a science. It is more of a process than an event.

Pastoral succession is unpredictable. It is messy, complex and complicated. It's never too early to start planning. Pastoral transition is not over when the new guy takes the helm. The complete process typically takes two or three years. So having this perspective is helpful even before you begin.

2. **Pray: Get on your knees.**

    In the complexity and unpredictability of this process, it can be easy to get discouraged. But you have something huge in your favor as you begin—it is this unique gift of prayer. Actually, it is not a huge something that you have in your corner. It is a huge *Someone*! God is certainly not unaware of your situation. He will not be surprised that you are looking for your next pastor. If Jesus said, "I *will* build my church, and the gates of Hades will not come against it," He certainly is more than capable of blessing you in your succession plan. He loves it when we recognize and acknowledge our limitations and entrust this to Him in prayer.

3. **Plan: Get ready.**

    A truism regarding pastoral succession is if you fail to plan, you may as well plan to fail. Here's part of why pastoral leadership transition does not go well: Approximately 25% of denominational pastors will retire, but have no retirement plan, and 25% of denominational pastors do not ever *plan* to retire. Most pastors and churches simply are not ready for transition! The outgoing pastor and the congregation must be prepared to answer the following questions:

- Am I emotionally ready?

- Am I professionally ready?

- Am I relationally ready?

- Am I spiritually ready?

- Am I physically ready?

- Am I financially ready?

While there are times when the outgoing pastor is indeed ready, nobody else in the church or organization is ready. What is honestly worse is when the board or staff is ready for the pastor to leave, but the pastor is *not*!

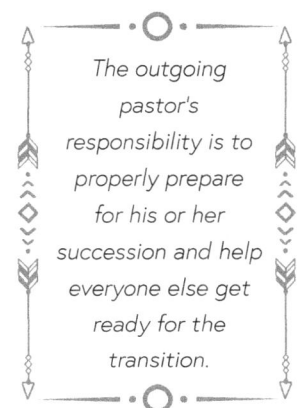

The outgoing pastor's responsibility is to properly prepare for his or her succession and help everyone else get ready for the transition.

The outgoing pastor's responsibility is to properly prepare for his or her succession and help everyone else get ready for the transition. This starts with the new pastor coming in (the "not-one-size-fits-all" comment earlier comes in here). Sometimes the outgoing pastor has someone on staff who they believe is the right successor. Sometimes, they might think this, but the staff or board might think differently. Maybe the board and staff feel they have the right successor, but the outgoing pastor does not think so. Perhaps, no one on the staff is a possible candidate.

In the best and most healthy of situations, the outgoing pastor can get the pastor coming in the readiest. The outgoing pastor should pour into their successor every possible bit of information they can, including but not limited to the history, culture, personality, valleys and mountaintops, personal hopes and even fears. There is some debate about how long the transition should be. However, whatever length of time that is chosen, make the best of the time to prepare the new pastor for leading well.

4. **Communicate: Get the word out.**

   The following series of communications are a *must* for a smooth succession:

   - Communication with God and family. How is this going? How am I feeling? What are my concerns?

- Communication with the incoming pastor must remain open. Even after the current pastor is gone, there should still be opportunity for open communication.

- Communication with the board of trustees is a must. This is another "no-one-size-fits-all" area. The board has to ensure, as best as they can, that the pastor going out does not develop the attitude that, "I will not have anything to do with this process." This is not a healthy position to place the incoming pastor in. When the outgoing pastor and the board have strong lines of communication with the incoming pastor, it spills over into the attitude of the congregation toward their new pastor.

- A significant concern/decision is how the staff would view the outgoing pastor once their departure has been communicated to the congregation and the incoming pastor has been onboarded. Decisions must be made in advance regarding when the incoming pastor occupies the pastoral office, what the outgoing pastor will be doing during the transition period, and at what time the congregation will begin taking direction from the incoming pastor.

- Over-communicate to the congregation about this transition through frequent emails and newsletters. Make many public comments in the middle of the transition.

5. **Humility and Honor: Get over yourself.**

This last step especially applies to the relationship between the outgoing and incoming pastors. The relationship between these two is one of the most essential factors in finding success. At the end of the day, pastors are simply God's servants. Therefore, we trust that God will continue to build His church. This should leave the outgoing pastor with enough humility to know that no matter who is leading, the church is in good hands because she's in God's hands.

6. **A Time of Refreshing and Renewal for All**

There must be a time where the new pastor and congregation gather together for a time of conversation, healing, restoration, getting to know one another, and building relationships based

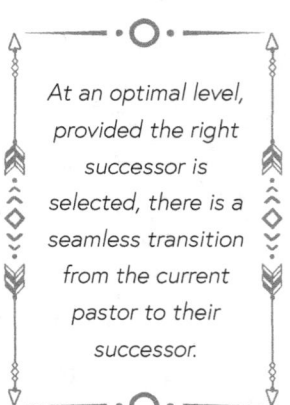

At an optimal level, provided the right successor is selected, there is a seamless transition from the current pastor to their successor.

on healed mindsets and not faulty perceptions. Group Therapy is a way to receive as a unified body foundation for forward progression. More often than not, we find out who leaders are based on sermons and teaching, and they find out about us based on how we respond. Group Therapy will be a time where everyone is on the same playing field and gathering together for fruitful dialogue and discussion regarding the past (outlooks, mindsets, preferences, etc.), the present (how it looks, what needs to take place, how things should be handled, what are the fears moving forward, and what God says about purpose and progress of transition), and the future (are we ready, will we allow movement to happen, will we let go of personal frustrations and preferences, will we see the transition through, and will we allow new leadership to actually lead, and will new leader have consistent accountability, not just to the people, but to God himself.)

The history of pastoral change in the Black church has caused much consternation for the congregation. Often, the church is without a pastor for a substantial period of time, causing a reduction in worship attendance, a decline in finances, and ministry cessation. To avoid this phenomenon from occurring, it is highly recommended that churches develop a pastoral succession plan. At an optimal level, provided the right successor is selected, there is a seamless transition from the current pastor to their successor.

This work was conducted to galvanize and institutionalize the process of pastoral succession in the life of Faith Church and abroad. It is hoped that the replicable model of pastoral succession developed by this project will be adopted by other churches as the necessity of pastoral change becomes a reality for the church; and it will.

ABOUT THE AUTHOR

While many leaders pursue accolades, awards and applause, he's solely in full pursuit of purpose fulfillment. Most passionate about seeing individuals healed, whole and prosperous in every area of their lives, Dr. Jason Moseley is on a mission to empower everyone he encounters to become the best version of themselves and live the abundant life God promised. Intentional about helping people heal mentally, emotionally and spiritually, Dr. Moseley serves not only as minister, but mentor, to many as he works diligently to instill God-fidence in people worldwide.

Reared in the church since childhood, his astounding affection for God and His people is unmatched. Raised by a mother who was well known for her writing and editing gifts, Dr. Moseley doesn't fall far from the tree with the launch of his debut book project, *Forward in Faith: How to Plan & Prepare for Successful Pastoral Transition.* Understanding the weight of pastoral transitions firsthand, through this project, he strives to help pastoral leaders and parishioners alike uphold a standard of holiness, purity and dignity as they experience transitions in leadership. Using a combination of historical, biblical and practical applications to explain succession planning in the religious sector, he argues how important it is for churches to plan for the future, so that ministry transitions are seamless.

As the senior pastor of Aijalon Baptist Church, Dr. Moseley is anointed and appointed for such a time as this. Holding a bachelor's degree in criminal justice from the University of Phoenix, Dr. Moseley furthered his education at Ashland Theological Seminary where he went on to earn a Master of Arts in Counseling degree. In 2023, Dr. Moseley earned his Doctor of Ministry degree from Payne Theological Seminary with a concentration in Transformational Preaching. And as the mission of Aijalon Baptist states, Dr. Moseley is crystal clear on his lifetime assignment: to acquire souls, build healthy families, and cultivate hearts for ministry.

Dr. Moseley and his wife Anita are the proud parents of two charming young men, Jeremiah and Caleb, as well as a beautiful young lady named Bella. For booking or speaking engagements, email admin@drjmoseley.org or visit drjmoseley.org.

BIBLIOGRAPHY

Archer, Gleason, Jr. *A Survey of Old Testament* Introduction. 3rd. ed. Chicago: Moody Press, 1994.

Armstrong, M. A Handbook of Human Resource Management Practice 9th Edition. London, UK: Cambrian Printers, 2003.

Arterbury, Andrew E. W. H. Bellinger, Jr, and Derek S. Dodson. *Engaging Christian Scriptures*. Grand Rapids, MI: Baker Academic, 2014.

Allen, KA., Fortune, K. C. & Arslan, G. (2021). "Testing the social-ecological factors of school belonging in native-born, first-generation, and second-generation Australian students: A comparison study." *Soc Psychol Educ*, 24, 835–856. Accessed September 15, 2022, https://doi.org/10.1007/s11218-021-09634-x.

Botella-Carrubi, D. & Gonzalez-Cruz, T. (2019). Context as a provider of key resources of key resources for succession: A case study of sustainable family firms. *Sustainability*, 11. 1873. Accessed September 15, 2022. https://doi.org/10.33 90/su11071873.

Bratcher, Robert G., and Barclay Moon Newman. *A Translator's Handbook on the Book of Joshua*. UBS Handbook Series. London, NY; New York: United Bible Societies, 1983.

Brown, Raymond E. *An Introduction to the New Testament*. New York, NY: Doubleday, 1997.

Burkett, R. K. (1978). Black Redemption: Churchmen Speak for The Garvey Movement. First Edition. Philadelphia, PA: Temple University Press, 1978.

Bunton, P. (2019). Reflexivity in practical theology: reflections from studies of founders' succession in Christian organizations. *Practical Theology*, 12(1). https://doi.org/10.1080/1756073X.2019.1575039

Butler, Trent C. *Joshua* 1–12. Edited by Nancy L. deClaissé-Walford. Second Edition. Vol. 7a. Word Biblical Commentary. Grand Rapids, MI: Zondervan, 2014.

Cantalamessa, Raniero. "'The Righteousness of God Has Been Manifested': The Fifth Centenary of the Protestant Reformation, an Occasion of Grace and Reconciliation for the Whole Church." *Journal of ecumenical studies* 53, no. 3 (2018): 423–435.

Cassidy, James J. God's Time for Us: Barth's Reconciliation of Eternity and Time in Jesus Christ. Bellingham, WA: Lexham Press, 2016.

Dudley, C. S. & Ammerman, T, N. (1998).

Eilam, G., & Shamir, B. (2005). Organizational change and self-concept threats. *The Journal of Applied Behavioral Science*, 41(4), 399-421. Accessed September 15, 2022. https://doi.org/10.1177/0021886305280865.

Farah, B., Elias, R., Clercy, C. & Rowe, G. (2020). "Leadership succession in different types of organizations: What business and political successions may learn from each other. *The Leadership Quarterly*, 31(1). https://doi.org/10.1016/j.leaqua.2019.03.004.

Fellows, Richard G, and Alistair C Stewart. "Euodia, Syntyche and the Role of Syzygos: Phil 4:2–3." *Zeitschrift für die Neutestamentliche Wissenschaft und die Kunde der älteren Kirche* 109, no. 2 (2018): 222–234.

Friedman, E. (1985). Generation to generation: Family process in Church and Synagogue. New York, NY: Guilford Press, 2011.

Frykholm, Amy. "A Time to Split?" *The Christian Century (1902)* 131, no. 8 (2014): 22.

Gates, H. L. Jr. (2021). The Black Church: This Is Our Story This Is Our Song. New York, NY: Penguin Press, 2021

Giambatista, R. C., Rowe, W. G., & Riaz, S. (2005). Nothing succeeds like succession: A critical review of leader succession literature since 1994. *The Leadership Quarterly*, 16(6), 963-991. https://doi.org/10.1016/j.leaqua.2005.09.005.

Gordon, F. Bruce. *Zwingli: God's Armed Prophet*. New Haven, CT: Yale University Press, 2021.

Grandy, G. (2013), "An exploratory study of strategic leadership in churches. *Leadership and Organization Development Journal*, 34(7), 616-638, 2013. Accessed September 15, 2022, https://doi.org/10.1108 /LODJ-08-2011-0081.

Grusky, O. Administrative succession in formal organizations. *Social Forces*, 39(2), 105. September 15, 2022, 1960, Accessed September 15, 2022. https://doi.org/10.108   6/223507.

_____. Managerial succession and organizational effectiveness. *American Journal of Sociology*, 69(1), 21-31, 1963. Accessed September 15, 2022, https://doi.org/ 10.1086/223507.

Haughton, J., Takemoto, M. L. Schneider, J., Hooker, S. P., Rabin, B., Brownson, R. C., & Arredondo, E. M. (2020). Identifying barriers, facilitators, and implementation strategies for a faith-based physical activity program. *Implementation Science Communications*, 1, 51, 2020. Accessed September 15, 2022. https://doi.org /10.1186/s43058-020-00043-3

Harmon, B., Blake, C., Armstead, C., James, H. "Intersection of identities: Food, role, and the African American pastor." *Appetite*, 67, 2013. Accessed September 15, 2022. https://doi.org/10.1016/j.appet.2013.03.007.

Harmon, B. E., Strayhorn, S., Webb, B. L., & Hébert, J. R. "Leading God's people: Perceptions of influence among African American pastors." *Journal of Religion and Health*, 57(4), 1509–1523, 2018. Accessed September 15, 2022. https://doi.org/10.1007/s10943-018- 0563-9

Heller, T. (Conversion process in leadership succession: A case study. *The Journal of Applied Behavioral Science*, 25(1), 65-77, 1989. Accessed September 15, 2022. https://doi.org/10.1177/0021886389251005.

Hess, Richard S. "Joshua: An Introduction and Commentary." Vol. 6. *Tyndale Old Testament Commentaries*. Downers Grove, IL: InterVarsity Press, 1996.

Howard, David M., Jr. "Joshua." Vol. 5. *The New American Commentary*. Nashville, TN: Broadman & Holman Publishers, 1998.

Johnson, G. *Leader shift: One becomes less while another becomes more*. Indianapolis, IN: Moeller Printing, Inc. 2013.

Kinnaman, David, "How Pastors Plan to Improve Their Churches," *The Barna Group*. Accessed September 15, 2022, www.barna.org/congregations-articles/ 560-how-pastors-plan-to-improve-their-churches.

Lincoln, E. C. & Mamiya, L. C. The Black Church in The African American Experience. Durham, NC: Duke University Press, 1990.

Longnecker, Bruce W. and Todd D. *Still. Thinking Through Paul*. Grand Rapids, MI: Zondervan, 2014.

Man-Stealing and Slavery Denounced by the Presbyterian and Methodist Churches: Together with an Address to All the Churches. Boston, MA: 1834.

McBeth, H. Leon. *The Baptist Heritage*. Nashville, TN: Broadman Press, 1987.

Miller, Emily McFarlan. "After Years of Debate, Conservatives Split from the United Methodist Church," *The Washington Post*. Last modified May 6, 2022. Accessed September 15, 2023, https://www.washingtonpost.com/religion/2022/05/06/after-years-loud-debate-conservatives-quietly-split-united-methodist-church/.

Olson, Roger E. *The Story of Christian Theology*. Downers Grove, IL: InterVarsity Press, 1999.

Pettegree, Andrew. *Brand Luther*. New York, NY: Penguin Books, 2015.

Manala, M. J. "A triad of pastoral leadership for congregational health and wellbeing: Leader, manager and servant in a shared and equipping ministry. *Hervormde Teologiese Studies*, 66(2), 1–6, 2010. Accessed September 15, 2022. https://doi.org/10.4102/hts.v66i2.875

Mangaliso, M, M, & Masango, M. "The challenge of pastoral succession in African independent Pentecostal churches." *HTS Teologiese Studies/Theological Studies*, 76(2), 2020. Accessed September 15, 2022, https://doi.org/10.4102/zhts.v76i2. 6265.

Masenya, M. J. (2021). "Caught between the sacred and the secular: The Pentecostal pastor as a leader in a world in constant flux." *Missionalia*, 49(1), 115-132, 2021. Accessed April 2, 2023. https://doi.org/10.7832/49-0-425.

Massey, F., & McKinney, S. Church Administration in The Black Perspective. Revised Edition. Valley Forge, PA: Judson Press, 2003.

Matshobane, M. M. & Masango, M. The challenge of pastoral succession in African independent Pentecostal churches. *HTS Teologiese Studies/Theological Studies*, 76(2), a6265, 2020. Accessed September 1, 2022. https://doi.org/10.4102/hts.v76 i2.6265.

Mdletye, M. A., Coerzee, J., & Ukpere, W. I. "The reality of resistance to change behavior at the department of correctional services of South Africa." *Mediterranean Journal of Social Sciences*, 5(3), 2014, Accessed September 15, 2022. https://doi.org/10.5901/mjss.2014v5n3p548

Mead, L. B. *A Change of Pastors. And How It Affects Change in The Congregation*. Washington, DC: Rowman & Littlefield, 2012.

Michaels, Cari, Linda Blake, Anna Lynn, Teale Greylord, and Sara Benning. "Mental Health and Well-Being Ecological Model." *Center for Leadership Education in Maternal & Child Public Health*, University of Minnesota–Twin Cities. April 18, 2022. Accessed September 15, 2022. https://mch.umn.edu/resources/mheco model/.

Neely-Fairbanks, S. Y., Rojas-Guyler, L., Nabors, L., & Banjo, O. "Mental illness knowledge, stigma, help-seeking behaviors, spirituality and the African American church." *American Journal of Health Studies*, 33(4), 162-174, 2018. Accessed September 15, 2022. https://doi.org/10.47779/ajhs.2018.69

Njoroge, J. K. & Mwangi, J. "Assessing factors affecting pastoral leadership transition in churches: A case of evangelical churches in molo sub-county." *International Journal of Advances Research and Review*, 3(9), 58-72, 2018. Accessed September 15, 2022.

Oswald, Roy and James and Ann Heath. *Beginning Ministry Together: The Alban Handbook for Clergy Transitions.* Herndon, VA: The Alban Institute, 2003.

Parker, G. (2018). "Succession planning.) *Public Garden*, 33(4), 10.

Phillips, W. B. Pastoral Transitions: From Endings to New Beginnings. New York, NY: Alban Institute Publication, 1988.

Reed, L. S. *Planning in The Small Church: Focusing on Gifts to Fulfill God's Call.* N.P., L. S. Reed, 2020.

Ritchie, M. Succession planning for successful leadership: Why we need to talk about succession planning!" *Management in Education*, 34(1), 2020.

Robinson, M. A., Jones-Eversley, S., Moore, S. E., Ravenell, J., & Adedoyin, A. C. "Black male mental health and the Black church: Advancing a 107 collaborative partnership and research agenda." *Journal of Religion and Health*, 57(3), 1095–1107, 2018. Accessed September 15, 2022. https://doi.org/10.1007/s10943-018-0570-x.

Rothwell, W. J. *Effective Succession Planning: Ensuring Leadership Continuity and Building Talent from Within* (3rd ed.). New York, NY: AMACOM, 2005.

Sherrer, M., Rezania, D. "A scoping review on the use and effectiveness of leadership coaching in succession planning." *International Journal of Theory, Research, and Practice*, 13(2), 2020.

Smith, M. D. (2009). *Transitional Ministry: A Time of Opportunity*. New York, NY: Church Publishing, 2009.

Son, A. "Anxiety as a main cause of church conflicts based on Bowen family systems theory." *Journal of Pastoral Care & Counseling*, 73(1), 9–18, 2019, Accessed September 15, 2022. https://doi.org/10.1177/1542305018822959.

Steinke, P.L. *How Your Church Family Works: Understanding Congregations As Emotional Systems*, Herndon, VA: Alban Institute, 2006.

Tucker, C. A. "Succession planning for academic nursing." *Journal of Professional Nursing*, 36(5), 334-342, 2020.

Vanderbloemen, W., & Bird, W. *Next: Pastoral Succession That Works*. Ada, MI: Baker Books. 2018.

Woudstra, Marten H. "The Book of Joshua." *The New International Commentary on the Old Testament*. Grand Rapids, MI: Wm. B. Eerdmans Publishing Co., 1981.

Wright, Bryant. *Succession: Preparing Your Ministry for The Next Leader*. Nashville, TN: B&H Books, 2022.